The INTENTIONAL *Life*

THE
INTENTIONAL
Life

CONNECTING DOTS...
OF PATTERN FOR CLARITY

S. Michelle ROSS

ISBN 979-8-88955-801-9 (softcover)
ISBN 979-8-88955-802-6 (eBook)

Cover and Book Design /Layout D'Edge Media

Edited by Althea Duren / ayebeeduren@gmail.com

Printed in the U.S.A

Dedication of Book:

To God for tasking me with this enormous task, for trusting in what He put in me and the retrieval process. To my husband, Brandon, for consistently providing for our family, which made Chef Chelles, LLC possible. Finally, Jay, your birth ushered me into ALL the work that God has birthed out of me. You have no idea how you changed my life for the better. Although you had no choice in the matter, just your existence forced me to move when I did not want to, could not, or did not know how. Your life gave me LIFE…thank you!

Foreword

It was a rainy, bleak day in Fort Myers, South Florida. We were holding Bible Study in a little restaurant when in walked this young lady dressed in a hat and coat carrying an umbrella. She made herself comfortable at the back and listened intensely to everything that was said. Surprisingly, she came back. This is how we met **S. Michelle Ross** and the rest is history.

Many people have come into and have left our lives since we have been pastoring for almost 20-plus years. Each of these individuals provided their unique experiences, abilities, and talents. **Michelle** is one of many who has constantly enhanced the New Alpha Worship Center Church family.

We owe God a significant debt of gratitude for placing this devoted servant and Christ-follower in our midst. **Michelle** radiates a strong desire for others to find their true calling in life and contribute to the growth of God's kingdom. These are her seven (7) steps of change:

1. **Acknowledgement**
2. **Illumination**
3. **Clarity**
4. **Intervention**
5. **Practice**
6. **Relapse**
7. **Change**

And they all connect.

In the Ecclesiastes book King Solomon penned, we read, "Let us hear the conclusion of the whole matter: Fear God, and keep his commandments: for this is the whole duty of man" (Ecclesiastes 12:13).

Also, in Luke 12:5, Jesus says, "But I will forewarn you whom ye shall fear: Fear him, which after he hath killed hath power to cast into hell; yea, I say unto you, Fear him."

In accordance, people who reject God's gift to humanity, Jesus Christ, will face judgment from God and eternal separation from Him. While God does not desire for any of His creation to be divided, He does desire for us to revere Him.

God has demanded obedience from the beginning. God gives commandments rather than making suggestions, which is a significant difference. Man was made to rule over everything that God had made, as well as to live forever. However, he did not realize that the all-knowing God has human beings' best interests at heart because like many people today, man was unable to grasp the broad picture.

In her masterpiece, **Michelle** masterfully addresses what and how God meant for man to live. She has used the anointing to stitch the reader's heart together after dissecting the Bible like a trained surgeon would with a knife.

So many times, we stick to the way we have always done things just because that is what we know. We make purposeful decisions and create boundaries primarily based on our past experiences. What this book will do, I believe, is enlighten you on how to be more intentional about what goes into the body, how you spend your time and money, and also how to better understand oneself using biblical principles.

Wasting purpose and potential is the saddest thing that can happen. Unfortunately, many people go through life never reaching their full potential or even close to it. There are several reasons for this, but I think the main one is that they have never had a life coach or mentor to help them connect the dots. They navigate life blindly, much like a person in the dark.

We weren't made by God to be mediocre, rather, He made us to be excellent. Living the Intentional Life is a great way to begin that process.

Pastors Errol and Angela Williams

Introduction

Behavior modification allows us to focus our attention and energy in an intentional effort of a task (behavior). It is the narrowing down of a broad category to its smallest denominator. It provides an opportunity to zero in on a specific task that has been identified as needing attention. That task can be anything from wearing make-up to surrendering our lives to God. It is the identification of the task and honing in on the what, how, when, why and where the task needs adjusting.

The words "behavior modification" in itself isolates behavior as the focus of scrutiny. Normally we do not notice our behavior because we are busy manifesting behavior. But God is after transformation from the inside out. When we accept Jesus as our personal Savior, He plants a seed of His holiness in us. That seed must be welcomed and allowed to reign over our very own will. That is, if the goal is to surrender to His will.

God calls all of us to a place of discipleship. He does not call the equipped (the ready, skilled, etc.), He equips the called. In Genesis 12:1-3, you see how God told Abraham to leave everything he knew, to "go from your country, your people and your father's household" (New International Version) to become a great nation. That same requirement is for every one of us. We must be willing to leave behind all that we value just as Abraham did for what God has for us.

We must be equipped (trained/taught) for the testimony God is writing in our lives. He has given each of us a lifetime to walk towards the perfection (Jesus's life on earth) that He has set before us. Our lifetime is already predetermined as His words states in Hebrews 9:27, "It is appointed to men once to die." Although we do not know how much time He has given each of us, what we do with our time should be focused.

Ephesians 4:1-16 is a good starting point. Verse 16 embodies the work we have been called to. The whole body depends on Christ, and …[through/ by whom] all the parts of the body are joined and held together. Each part [supporting joint/ligament] does its own work [performs its function] to make the whole body grow and be strong with [to build itself up in] love (Expanded Bible). That work CANNOT be done to God's standard outside of Him!

Colossian 3:12-15 reinforces what we have been called to do, of which we can do none of it in our selves. We need Christ! We simply need to learn to first acknowledge our own behavior and its deficiencies as we cry out to Christ for wisdom, allowing God to walk us away from all we have learned, chosen, and valued in exchange for Him. God knew when He called us what He was calling us to and what we needed to be successful in for the completion of our task.

We, on the other hand, do not know the full scope of the task, what we are capable of, nor how to complete the task but we struggle to relinquish control in every way. Even though God knew what would happen, He was the one who gave us dominion. God knows everything in its entirety! He knows our struggle: to give our lives over to a God who we cannot see, but must believe, and does not bend to our will, ever!

We do not go from self-reliance to total dependence (obedience) on Christ in one moment. Process is the way of change which none of us can escape. We are born into an evil and wicked world system (our desires). Jesus came before us to show how we are to navigate through this system. He is the perfection of what God wanted for us all before the fall of man in the garden. Jesus was sent just like you and I are as Christians.

The great commission in Matthew 28:19-20 is Jesus telling His disciples to do as He had demonstrated to them. He himself came down from heaven not to do His own will but the will of Him that sent Him (John 6:38). He was sent for multiple reasons, one being an example for us to follow, and another that He might destroy the works of the devil (1 John 3:8).

God is very intentional (purposeful/deliberate) in His plans. He knew when He made man that they would choose to eat from the tree He told them not to. Knowing that He had another plan, Jesus was in the bosom of the Father (John 1:18). God sent Jesus to die a horrific and brutal death as an innocent man, knowing that His shed blood would cover the sins of those coming after Him.

Jesus chose to be obedient throughout the entire process, the humiliating accusations, the beatings, the disbelief, the judgmental stares and words, so that God would be glorified. That level of discipline does not just happen even when you want it, are focused on being it, or because you say so. That level of discipline requires supernatural intervention.

To position oneself for this supernatural intervention one must start the process of identifying and surrendering one's will.

The Intentional life is the start of that process. The power to defeat the devil is in yielding your will to that of the Holy Spirt, which is a choice. All the ability the enemy (the devil) has was given to him by his Creator. The mere fact that God created a thing gives Him an advantage over His creation. As a creator you know the weaknesses of your creation, what it can and cannot do, how it moves, and why. God is that creator and He has called us to be His representative in the earth. If you are to do His will, you must first recognize your inability to do it without Him and without change.

The person you are today will not be the same person who finishes this journey, should you embark. The Intentional Life will allow you to see yourself in ways you have dismissed, overlooked, excused or are downright delusional about. This process will teach you how to look at yourself through a lens you have avoided. It will allow you a guided path back to where things changed or were initiated. It provides a systematic approach to looking at your behavior patterns that you have labeled, "That's just who I am." It will give you a place to start and means of holding you accountable to yourself.

This is not something that can be done in one sitting of reading. This will require reflection, studying, confrontation, isolation, acceptance, and forgiveness. If and when you decide to accept the call on your life, The Intentional Life is an excellent tool to use to start being Intentional in an intentional way by trusting in the God who made you!

Contents

CHAPTER 1

Process of Emotional Scarring

Pliability is having the quality of being easily bent. Once we enter the world as infants, everything about us physically, mentally, and spiritually are all very pliable. As we age, we become more rigid. This rigidness affects all areas of our lives and gives permission to allow or deny movement when exposed to any new stimuli. Our rigidness will or will not allow us to try to take part in innovation.

The fallow ground spoken of in Hosea 10:12 refers to that rigidity of our untouched ground in all areas. It is the stiffness of our stance on allowing innovation into our territory. Fallow ground is soil that has been untouched for a season. It is settled and unchallenged. When a farmer decides he wants to plant in that soil he must break it up to get it to a soft pliable state, ready to receive and nurture seeds.

The same is true of our hearts, unchallenged until we heed the call of God. That soil of our heart, mind, and soul has been unchallenged by the things of God, subject only to the things we have been exposed to. When we are shaped by this world system as we grow, those belief systems become our fallow ground. It is that compacted untouched soil that must be broken up, in our hearts, minds, and souls. The tightly packed soil is unable to receive anything. Even rainwater struggles to invade its layers. It must be broken up to receive the seed of God's word. Fallow ground can be formed as a result of trauma.

THE INTENTIONAL LIFE

The introduction of a trauma can occur at any point in our lives. When we are young the impact of emotional trauma has a much greater impact over the totality of our life, establishing filters from which we will view our future. Filters initiate in our behaviors just as rings appear in the center of tree trunks. If you take a slice out of tree's trunk, it will show us the seasons and weather conditions of its growth. A light-colored ring represents growth during the spring and early summer, while the dark rings represent growth in the late summer and fall. One light ring plus one dark ring equals one year of the tree's life. The rings also tell us the weather conditions during each season of growth. For instance, tree rings grow wider in warm seasons and thinner in wet years, even drought times show up as lack of growth ("What Can Trees Tell Us About Climate Change?").

To make a comparison, the conditions in nature are filters which allow trees to grow. The same is true for us in the sense of seeds or information once anchored into our soil (soul). Once these seeds are anchored, they grow to become filters which dictate our growth (e.g., behavior, choices) in the same way seasons and weather conditions dictate tree growth.

The enemy desires to begin the filtering process in infancy. If he can snare or scar us at an early age, the deeper and more secure is his anchor, keeping us locked in place, bound in fear, hopelessness, and despair. He wants us to be his servants for a lifetime and he takes every opportunity to keep us bound. His attempt to keep us bound is established from the initiation of filters, to the internalization of those filters, then the formation of habits that cements those filters, and finally, the death of innocence altogether.

Initiation

Children come into this world dependent on others to meet their needs. The way their needs are met will begin to establish filters of how the child will view others in the world, how or if they trust, how they define good and bad, right, and wrong and what love is, how they view themselves and others…in other words, everything about their development! Therefore, God tells parents to train up a child in the way they should go in Proverbs 22:6. They need the training to prepare for the battle they will face with our adversary. The sooner the training begins the better.

Children are sponges absorbing everything that occurs around them. Every emotional connection or the lack thereof establishes these filters from which they will view life. These established standards become their default settings (muscle memory, automatic response system) or foundation on which the child will build. It is the main reason to do things the way God prescribes. His way guarantees success in defeating the enemy within this system.

When a man and a woman get married and produce a child, that child is subjected to its parents' experiences and knowledge. What they value is passed along to their child and the same of what they do not value. They bring with them their tainted established filters from which they teach their child, adding to the child's foundation. Neither parent may have recognized their filters nor from where they came, remaining in need of allowing God to break up the fallow ground of their foundation that was laid by their flawed parents.

Each of us are born to imperfect parents consequently we all need to have the foundation of who we have grown into to be broken up and rebuilt on the true foundation which is the word of God. This is true for those who have even grown up in homes where the word of God was spoken. All of us come to God with a personality shaped in iniquity (Psalm 51:5). We teach the word of God built on our understanding, knowledge, and interpretation of reading the word. The Bible tells us in 2 Corinthians 3:6 that "the letter killeth, but the spirt giveth life." As we mature, we learn to trust God and the Holy Spirit.

By the time we know better, our kids may have left the house, and many things may have transpired. The things that we may have thought were true may not have been "the truth." For example, some people believe they do not need to be baptized after they accept Christ. They believe that Jesus was baptized for them but in Acts 2:38, we read otherwise. Believing in our heart and confessing with our mouth is what grants salvation, but baptism is our first obedient act of faith. It is the first of many acts of being obedient by faith. Many individuals who hold this belief do so because it was introduced to them at an infancy stage of belief and/or development. Even though they may have read Acts 2:38, they continue anchored in their truth.

THE INTENTIONAL LIFE

The weight of information, knowledge, experience and observation poured into a child during their innocent years is comparable to the weight of ten male elephants stacked atop each other. The child did not ask for the information, and the parents might not be aware the child has the information nor what should have been done, especially if they too had to endure similar behavior from their parents.

Some parents see it as a rite of passage for their children to learn on their own or "to make do." God did not intend for that to happen when He produced children through the union of a man and a woman. His word says in Proverbs 22:6, to "train up a child in the way they should go." If we do not train our children the "foolishness that is bound up in their hearts," (Proverbs 22:15) will be their teacher. That foolishness must be curtailed by discipline (training) so when they explore (prodigal time) they have their training to guide them back to a place of truth.

We are born selfish and need to be taught how to share and to think of others. Children will make everything about them. They do not understand everything is not about them, but in their world, it is. It is something we all enter this world system with, and we struggle the longest surrendering it.

When children are born, they demand our time and energy on schedule. They tell us when it is time to eat, sleep, and play. We, as parents, graciously embrace their time schedule until we start the process of teaching them ours. That is the point of disruption or intervention for the child. Now a demand is being placed on them to comply with something different than compared to what they have grown accustomed to doing.

This is their first lesson of thinking of others and the initiation of our roles as trainer. It is the necessary training they need to live in our world. That training or shaping is what they will need to surrender to God. We are to prepare them by shielding them from the enemy long enough for them to take up their own armor.

Internalization

Every piece of information that passes through our gates (our five senses) must be anchored somewhere to create a filter.

Connecting Dots of Pattern For Clarity

That somewhere is in the soil of our hearts, our soul which is where our intellect, will, and emotions are housed. Another way of thinking about it is as seeds dropped into soil for planting. The seed must be anchored into the soil for proper growth and development. If the seed is not properly anchored what happens to that information is as described in Matthew 13:1-9 and 18-23, the parable of the soils.

Each seed (information) must not just land on top of the soil but must be completely sheltered by the soil. The soil provides a place for the seed to receive nutrients, protection, and a place to grow (develop). As we read in Matthew, the other soils could not produce a filter because of where the seed (information) landed in proportion to the soil.

The seed that "fell by the wayside" produced nothing as it was eaten by birds, equivalent to a passing thought that we allow to fly away without much thinking. Seeds that "fell on stony places" is information that produced something (a behavioral or emotional response) quickly but was scorched by trails (the sun). This is equivalent to an emotional response in the moment but has no depth to sustain, similar to sexual attraction, intense but easily extinguished. "Some fell among thorns." The thorns represent the wickedness (pride) that is present in all of us that comes to choke any and everything contrary to itself.

Our internal process is very much like growing a tree. To grow a tree there must be a seed planted in good soil. As the seed is anchored into the soil, nurtured, and fortified by its environment, given time the tree will grow. As the tree grows stronger and bigger, removal of the tree becomes more arduous. The same is true of the "trees" (behavioral patterns) in our souls.

Our soul is what has been shaped by iniquities and cannot be trusted, and the anchoring process allows us a consistent pathway of retrieval. It is a singular dot that we may need to connect to another dot to get clarity of a random pattern of behavior we see in ourselves. Following the trail of dots back to the time, location, action, behavior, situation, and other circumstances of when the seed was anchored. Connecting these random dot patterns of behavior will lead us to the root of why we behave (believe, think, or act), giving us a clear pattern to disrupt should we desire to do so.

THE INTENTIONAL LIFE

Making the connection to the dots of behavior is essential to change in the same way it is essential to removing the stump and root system when a tree is cut down. If you only cut the limbs of a tree, the tree limbs will eventually regrow. Even if you cut the tree in half the stump will regrow the tree in time. But if you remove the roots of the tree, it will never return.

What we want to do is to uproot the entire process of how we do things, how we think, and how we behave, to do so the root system of our way of doing things must be removed. To remove the root, one must be able to identify the tree (e.g., behavior) by connecting the dots of pattern that led to the roots of said behavior.

In 2 Corinthians 10:5, we are told to "bring every thought captive to the obedience of Christ." To internalize this truth would look like taking the time to "fact check" every thought we have, bringing that thought to be measured against what the word of God says about it. The information could seem factual, but if it does not line up to what the word of God says about it, it is not the truth.

Any of us could have a thought that we are worthless. It may be a true feeling but it is NOT the truth about us. Ephesians 2:10 states, "We are His workmanship." Genesis 1:27 reminds us we are created in His image. God would not make a worthless image of Himself. It is a lie from the enemy we have believed that needs to be taken to Christ and fact checked. The earlier we incorporate this standard of capturing random thoughts and holding them up to God's word, the sooner it becomes a part of our automatic response system.

Once a thought (seed) is introduced, the internalization process has an opportunity to modify that thought. The thought will either be captured and measured against God's truth, or it is accepted as our truth. It will not just float around in our cosmic emotional atmosphere but land into one of the four "soil" conditions of our heart.

Similar to when building a house, the foundation is laid and then the walls are attached. We have never seen walls hanging in the air waiting for somewhere to land. The word of God is our foundation upon which everything about us is built on. If and when the house (our emotional development) was built and the foundation was not properly laid (abuse occurred), signs will show in all the areas of the house.

If the stove is not leveled, when baking all cakes will lean to one side. Walls will slowly separate making cracks along the walls, the evidence of poor foundation work.

The same can be said about our tell-tale signs of self-harm, low or no self-esteem, violence, promiscuity, and many more mental challenges. Instead of doing landscaping to these areas of concern (trees), we can kill the tree at the root. This is done by developing good skills based on the word of God to repair our foundation, correct those areas of need, and righting our house.

One of two things are done when trauma presents itself, either we implode or explode. To implode is to take vengeance out on ourselves internally by withdrawing. Withdrawing is concluding that we have no control over the trauma, so we go inward where we do have control. Thank God we cannot control all of our bodily functions but the ones we can are targeted, like eating, bathing, when to go to the bathroom, and the like. These functions bear the brunt of our internal assault such as intentionally choosing not to take a bath or eat. To explode is the opposite of implode, that is to take vengeance out on people, objects, and in other ways outside of ourselves. It is the unleashing of all emotions in an uncontrollable bout, completely at the mercy of the outpour for its duration. Exploding is also the result when we have not released the things that we have been carrying. Instead of releasing (confronting or acknowledging) them, we pretend they do not exist until we can hide them no longer. At that point, they simply erupt, causing unmitigated damage.

Without a history of regulating our emotions, we either hide them or allow them to control us. Rarely are we taught to allow the feeling to present itself fully and then decide on how to move on from what was felt. We are given clear parameters of acceptance for what those around us accept and do not accept and we are expected to fall in line. Stepping outside of that expectation makes us vulnerable, but a strong foundation in Christ makes us resilient. It is our safety net to learn to trust Him by internalizing His word which will comfort and correct the lies we have believed no matter how long they have been our truth.

THE INTENTIONAL LIFE
Habits

After we have internalized, we then begin exhibiting behaviors that support the new pattern of behavior (filter). For example, Adam and Eve opened the door of sin as a filter. The filter becomes the gate that everything after its established, must enter and exist, giving the filter dominance.

Anything that enters our gates passes through this new filter, in the same way we are all shaped in sin and cannot escape our sinful nature due to Adam's disobedience. We are all subject to the consequences of his choice. There is no way around it, no exceptions. All humans born are tainted with the same sinful makeup that Adam and Eve initiated. Even our "good" deeds are tainted with the evil of this world system (flesh) as described in Romans 7:18.

As the process continues, we totally lose sight of the original filter, creating normalcy defined by the new pattern of behavior. It now has become a part of the foundation of how/why everything that occurs after that point even exists. It has entered the automatic (habitual) response phase. In this phase we consistently build the same methodical pattern of behavior or response based on the new filter's standard. This methodical pattern making process has now become the steppingstone for everything that follows in its path.

Everything we interact with, in any form (e.g., an idea, a thought, a vision, a feeling) will pass through this standard of behavior (filter), encasing us into a standard we may not want and do not recognize as it takes control. The longer the standard goes unchallenged it reinforces itself, giving validity to our feelings and outcomes (behaviors).

The process of fortification occurs each time the original internalization is fed. It gives life and validation, strengthening its positions. To fortify something simply means to make it stronger. If you fortify wrong thinking it will become stronger, making it harder to combat.

The timing of the introduction of the thought aids in the internalization process. It does so by playing into fears already aligned with the time of day or night the thought was introduced. Attaching a feeling intensifies the process, cementing the thought in both our mind and emotions.

Let us look at an example of being told cats are evil (seed/filter) shortly after a frightening encounter with one. As interactions with other cats outside of the original trauma occurs, that now established filter that cats are evil is creating barriers, barriers that will challenge any new thought of cats not being evil. Those barriers will block other options such as an opinion, suggestions, and ideas, giving it supremacy. They can include imaginary and unrealistic visions of cat behavior, unsolicited thoughts, and situations designed by the enemy to create anxiety. Every interaction had near or around a cat will be viewed and assessed through the filter of cats are evil. Even hearing others talk about cats can trigger our built-in emotional response. A cat really does not have a chance to prove itself otherwise in the mind where this filter operates.

The filter becomes more fortified by any negative interactions with cats by acknowledging and confirming the fear of the original trauma. The trauma remains at a heightened state in our emotions as it is replayed in our consciousness. This replaying is keeping the pain fresh until its anchor has secured us in stagnation and avoiding remedy.

Once we are secured in stagnation that cats are evil, we avoid cats, holding onto the memory of our body's emotional response as a reminder. Avoiding the emotional response is what keeps us from venturing out for a remedy. We simply avoid the possibility of anxiety, staying locked in stagnation. We then become conditioned to manage our symptoms of avoidance by masking up, self-medicating, and finding other ways to avoid the root (initial thought).

The very way we view cats is now dictated by the original trauma and its fortification. Therefore, it is almost impossible for us to see a positive interaction with a cat without being premeditated. Every possible outcome is judged based on the pattern of behavior (filter), not the trueness of the actual situation. As mentioned, it is an automatic (habitual) response at this point. Our responses are so quick we do not notice them unless we are intentionally focusing on them. Even then it would not stop the emotional or physical response. We will just notice it occurred.

Death is the final step in the process of emotional scarring. As the process begins, death is the goal. For the trauma to successfully scar us, it must halt (kill off) the innocence which was in that space before the trauma was introduced. Using the cat scenario, before being told cats were evil, one would have never had a feeling one way or the other about cats. That space (untouched fertile soil) prior to the seed (the thought that cats are evil) being dropped into the soil of the consciousness of the individual, is their virtue.

Virtue is what is being put to death. No longer does innocence exist in that space. That virtuous soil has now been infiltrated with a seed. Once the thought (seed) was introduced that information is anchored in our soul (soil). When it was attached, it brought about death to the innocence.

To summarize the emotional scarring process, let us look at it as a virus. A virus needs a host to survive and reproduce to the point of destroying its host by halting its normal process. Imagine touching a doorknob contaminated with the flu virus then going back to continue eating an open bag of chips left on your desk. By licking your flu-infested fingers the virus has now entered your body (initiation). At this point you will not recognize nor show symptoms of the flu (trauma) because the flu can take up to four to five days to show any symptoms in the body.

Now that the virus has entered our body, it quickly moves on to the internalization phase. This step is identical to the processing of filters; the virus has become the filter. The virus has anchored itself inside of our body and forcing every healthy cell to pass through its filter, infecting them.

Similarly, signs of scaring do not show up in our behavior for months or years. Although the flu virus has invaded our body, its effects on our health have not presented themselves. What is occurring in our body without our knowledge is the virus which has attached itself to our cell duplication command center and has begun duplicating itself (creating a habit).

This process is similar to what we do when we mask up. We hide behind a mask which dictates our behavior and self-talk, teaching others how to treat us, and giving the false appearance that everything is well. Once the virus has reached its optimal capacity, we begin to feel its effects. This is also when the habit (behavior) is most noticeable.

Connecting Dots of Pattern For Clarity

Now we are experiencing symptoms such as body aches, fever, cough, sore throat, and headaches. These symptoms are our warning signs that something is going on inside of us. It is our body's notification that something has entered and altered our normal working system. Just like the time before the change was noticed in our health, we experience a similar time-lapse in our behavior. The decline of our physical health must warn us that the flu has invaded our operating system, or we would not know.

In the same way, we have symptoms like a runny nose for the flu, we have feelings alerting us of behavioral needs. Feelings are emotional warning signs for our behavioral needs. They are the body's alert system, notifying us that a new filter has been anchored in our soil which needs our attention. Like the rings of a tree when drought occurs, little growth happens during that season.

The virus has entered our body, anchoring itself to our cell control center where all healthy cells come and go, infecting each as they pass through. At this point, the flu has begun mass-producing itself by infecting healthy cells as they exit its filter. As a result of the infection (death) of each healthy cell, our internal struggle is becoming physically visible to those outside of us.

A problem we run into is our pride does not want us to change from its control. Our pride filter will begin to speak (self-talk) to us about how we know ourselves better than anyone else, we are good people, and other statements of validation. It aids in our deception, keeping us in a mask we want to shed but are unsure of how or when. Although our goal as a child of God is to move towards the truth of His word, in reality we have learned to live in our subpar conditions because leaving that comfort is scary and risky.

Relationships are breeding grounds for critiques, judgements, and observation. Some behaviors are masked better than others in relationships for various reasons. If one person is in the role of victim and another person is an enabler, this relationship can be successful at maintaining a comfortable level of dysfunction for both participants. They both are feeding into each other's dysfunctions, and neither are growing in either of those underdeveloped areas of need. Neither of them may even be aware of their areas of need without the influence of an outside source.

Someone outside of their relationship may be able to see the dynamic of their sickness. This is why we go see a doctor when our health is challenged. We need someone outside of us to judge the situation that we are so engrossed in. A physician will ask for your symptoms, looking for the root that is causing the symptoms. A doctor knows that the way we experience something does not necessarily mean it is the cause of the experience.

For instance, symptoms for liver disease are yellowing of the eyes and skin, and swelling in the legs and ankles. Unless someone had prior knowledge, they would not suspect their swelling ankles had anything to do with their liver failing. If those same symptoms occur in a person with knowledge of liver failure, they will make the connection between the symptoms and the diagnosis. Again, they are outside of the situation objectively viewing the symptoms described with known ailments.

We do not correctly connect behavior (symptoms) with our trauma because we have spent so much time and energy covering them up, hiding, or ignoring them. Having a trusted person in our lives can aid in making these necessary connections. In both cases, without intervention, the invader (flu virus or trauma), will continue to remake itself until it kills (halts/separate) its host.

If for some reason we still do not recognize or acknowledge that our consequences are connected to our behavior, the word of God will clear it up for us unequivocally. Simply reading the word of God with any level of consistency will reveal what our feelings and others have been trying to alert us of. His word will allow the scales to fall off our eyes (Acts 9:18). Then we will be able to clearly see that behavior which has been with us all the time.

God, through His word, will illuminate the situation for us so that we may see it and the process of our automatic response system will no longer blind us to our behavior. Once we can see and are able to acknowledge that there is a problem, then we can do something about it. This is when we can move from having no idea to where we decide what to do or if we want to do anything about it.

CHAPTER 2
The Shaping of our Character

Whatever God has given us as an assignment individually, we are going to suffer to bring it forth! Just think about how He makes diamonds. Diamonds are crystalized carbons that look like charcoal that is formed beneath the earth's surface. After years under the prefect conditions of heat and pressure, they erupt from their hiding place through some sort of natural disturbance ("How Are Diamonds Formed?"). They are most prized for their uniqueness, clarity, rarity, and hardness.

When you think you have a true stone there are ways to test it to ensure of its authenticity. Some of those tests include looking at the stone under ultraviolet (UV) light, seeing if it fogs, checking the stone for inclusions (small imperfections), or heating it up with fire.

As God's chosen vessels we too are prized for our uniqueness, clarity, rarity, and firmness (hardness). We are all made of the same substance (dirt, Genesis 2:7) but God designed each of us just a little differently. Each individual human is unique and rare, even if you are an identical twin. Twins may share a face, but God made sure they both have a uniqueness that even the other twin does not have. He gave each of us our own set of fingerprints. He in His supremacy made only one of each human because He values uniqueness and rarity.

THE INTENTIONAL LIFE

Each one of us was chosen before the foundation of the world was formed to do one job. God knew what He wanted and designed us particularly for that job before we even knew what we wanted to do. God specifically handpicked not only our parents but our lineage. It was foretold that Jesus would come through the line of David in John 7:42. The book of Chronicles and others maintain detailed records of the birth of significant males for that reason alone. Luke 3:36 takes us on a journey through the genealogical lineage back to Shem of Jesus's pedigree.

The same God who is able to bring forth our Redeemer with enormous detail and accuracy did the same for every other person He has selected for a task. Things only appear coincidental.

The formation of our soul through wickedness is what we have grown to embrace, which has not prepared us for what God has called us to do. Therefore, we must undergo discipline to have the necessary experiential knowledge of how to stand under the pressure of change. We are His "charcoal" being made into priceless heirlooms.

Remember Jesus was our example. He demonstrated with perfection how to live this life and complete His purpose. He showed us how we are to treat others, how to be angry and sin not, how to respond to adversity, and how to die. How we view His life's work will dictate how we move forward. It is how we internalize that work which brings the manifestation of His call on our lives. We all will go through our own unique process of heat and pressure throughout our lives. Learning from Christ as our ultimate example and those before us will aid in our understanding.

No one has been flawless to God's assignments except Jesus. We all make mistakes and have to be renewed in our thinking by ultimately giving up our will for God's prefect will. Similarly, we do not know what we are being called to until after we are called to serve. Each of us must learn to trust and obey God in the transformation process, yielding our ways and life story to the master storyteller, knowing that He has a story He wants our lives to tell.

This reshaping and renewing of our minds are processes we all must go through to complete the course set before us. The longer it takes us to recognize our calling and to yield to its necessary renewing, the harder it is to do something different. Individually we are not working up to the design of the manufacturer's standards. Therefore, by not answering the need in society, we are leaving gaping holes we were designed to fill.

God is shaping us into the image of Christ. Jesus during His time on earth was tried consistently by the enemy and through many different vessels (persons), Pharisees, chief priests, Sadducees (colleagues, Matthew 16:1-4), John the Baptist (Luke 7:19), and friends (John 6:42). If we are to be made in His image, we too must allow God to create in us a clean heart and renew a right spirit within us (Psalm 51:10).

We know from the word of God in Psalms 51:5 that we are shaped in iniquity (wickedness). That is the very shaping that we must sacrifice on the altar of God. God does not force this surrender process (change). He simply draws us closer to Him, allowing us to see our great need for Him. Through that process of drawing us through His grace and mercy, we desire to please Him. And the love that He gives us breaks the hold of wickedness just enough that we want to please Him more than ourselves.

The beauty of God is in our weakness His strength is perfected (2 Corinthians 12:9)! We simply do what we can, and God takes over giving welcome relief from straining to carry a load we were not designed to carry.

During this process, God is strengthening our resolve to move forward by allowing testing to help us to see patterns of behavior that were previously not visible to us. They give us a starting point of focus, connecting our consequences to our behavior. Testimonies come from the results of clear hindsight connections.

God knows how long we have carried these loads and how long it takes to build new habits of release. He teaches us through the process of application, replacing our way with His way. As we consistently do this, we are taking His yoke upon us (Matthew 11:29-30), defined as a crosspiece of wood fitted on the neck of an animal attached by traces (straps/chains), used to guide through working ("Yoke").

What we as people have come accustomed to doing when faced with pain (test) is to anesthetize it (medicate, cover up) in such forms as drugs, alcohol, humor, sarcasm, anger, making excuses, attacking people, and many other forms. But we must get in the habit of giving that pain to God, for as we starve our pride, we strengthen our spiritual muscles.

We anesthetize because we have not given it to God. What we do is cover up the bleeding until it soaks through the bandage, again revealing itself. We repeat this until a habit is formed, hiding the bleeding versus cauterizing the wound.

We only give our pain to God when we have exhausted all our options or we have learned how to do so. Once we are taught, the teaching is not beneficial unless it is applied. It is like building trust. We will question the process or person until satisfaction of all our questions consistently are provided.

He knows we fight hard against outside standards that differ from our belief systems, traditions, and habits. This leaves us stranded on an island of delusion (misunderstanding) with a dismantled bridge, sealed in a mausoleum of what we know only. It is a place of comfort that we do not want to leave to enter the unknown, so we stay.

Concession

Concession is when we surrender or concede to the demand to do something different. This can be when we finally acknowledge we feel the pull of the Holy Spirit in our lives. It can be the breaking point of hitting rock bottom or simply running out of options. Concession is the point we reach when we no longer deny the signs we have ignored.

Concession is difficult for us because we are made in the image of God. He gave us dominion to rule. He knows what we need and when we need it. As a result, God raises up vessels (individuals) to teach us how to come to Him. He knows the when, where, what, how, and who to use for any given time and for any given situation.

Getting to the point of concession for each of us can look very different. God has built a uniqueness into each of us by choosing our parents, how and where our parents grew up, with whom, with what and the like, which all influenced us. Parents can also be keys to unlocking strategies necessary for rebuilding the bridge previously ripped to pieces, beckoning us to cross.

A quiet person who manipulates by not talking may create conflict in his or her spouse who longs for communication. The process of concession may be for them to speak but because they have not had practice doing so, when they do speak their words may fumble out of their mouth without a care for how they may be received.

On the other hand, the concession for someone who is a talker or who frequently expresses how they feel about things, may need to remain quiet.

To know for certain what will work best for you as the individual requires you to draw closer to the One who knows all! God knows intricate details (dots of pattern) about each of us that should be considered. He knows what is best for us.

The issue we have is by the time we come to Christ we may have already built a foundation (crossed the bridge) on many wounds. At this point we may not have dismantled all the bridges, but have crossed over to our island of delusion. We begin living our lives in a way that creates self-reliance we do not know how to relinquish. We cannot comprehend a life dependent on a God we cannot see.

We struggle at the thought of a God who knows what we know about ourselves and yet fully accepts us. We have questions like, "How is it possible for Him to know everything about us and still love us?" and "Why would He want somebody like me?" These are the type of self-defeating questions that concession has to fight through. As concession fights, we would rather question God's methods than begin building the bridge to His understanding.

God does not waste anything He allows in our lives. What may work in one individual's life may not work in another's because of the many variables. God is the only one who can untangle the vastness of variables of individual circumstances.

The imaginary pain associated with crossing the bridge to God's understanding can be extremely uncomfortable, which is why we move quickly to alleviate it. By doing so we create a self-protection filter which overall winds up causing as much discomfort as it was designed to alleviate.

Not believing in God is not an answer, it is a starting place. Just because one does not study His word or even believe in Him does not mean His word is not valid. It is just like acknowledgement. A situation does not cease to exist because one does not acknowledge it, it just does not exist to that individual.

That individual is forfeiting an opportunity to move past what can be seen or how it is seen. In Proverbs 3:5, it is called "leaning on our own understanding." Take the law of gravity. If someone chooses to not believe in the law of gravity, the law does not cease to exist, nor does its effect on a person or object change. To prove it, one would simply throw a ball into the air or jump off a roof. The ball and the person will fall to the ground without fail.

Your mindset of the law of gravity will be challenged at the point of impact. However, your previous thought of the law of gravity now comes into question (is challenged). At that point you must reevaluate your previous choice. As you reevaluate your previous understanding (e.g., truth, belief, behavior, choice) you will need to make another choice. What you are choosing from is whether to continue in your understanding or to do something different.

Choosing to remain in your current understanding or to "do nothing" are both examples of how we activate our blinders. It is how we give ourselves permission without actually (consciously) saying "I am choosing to do the same thing," even though the relationship between behavior and consequence is evident. The activation of our blinders is how we get to the point of not seeing what is right in front of us. They take our focus off the actual relationship between our consequence and our behavior, placing it elsewhere such as on our feelings or by blaming others.

CHAPTER 3
Consequences

Behavior is anything that can be seen, heard, or measured. All behaviors have consequences and an antecedent. The antecedent comes before the behavior and the consequence immediately follows the behavior. Consequences are what drive our behavior (Webster #). They can be both positive and negative, immediate, and delayed. The severity and immediacy of the consequence determines whether a behavior will change, how quickly, or if at all. Even negative consequences can fuel a behavior, especially when the severity is tolerable. The consequence of going to jail is normally viewed as negative, but if you are homeless, it could fuel a crime spree.

Consequences occur in one of three ways: Natural, Logical, or Artificial (problem-solving).

Natural consequences are consequences that occur naturally without any additional intervention such as if you are running and you fall or trip (consequence) or lose weight (consequence) after reducing food intake. These are consequences that just happen naturally based on the behavior before it. There is nothing additional. This type of consequence will naturally occur after a behavior.

Logic is a way of thinking about something, and logical consequences are consequences that have been logically prearranged to increase or decrease a behavior. They are consequences that make sense. They follow a logical pattern of acceptance per a norm. It is the "if you do this, I will give you that" way of thinking. We work, and it is logical for us to expect payment for our services based on our work compensation norm.

It is the previous experience or history (way of thinking or logic) that dictates the logical consequences. Logical consequences differ between the Old Covenant (Old Testament) and the New Covenant (New Testament).

God told Adam what the consequence would be if he chose to eat from the tree, "...thou shalt surely die" (Genesis 2:17). Logically thinking, Adam had the mind of Christ. He was a perfect being made in the image of God, so he knew death would be separation from God.

The enemy (serpent in Genesis 3:4) knew that Adam and Eve were completely innocent and gave them something to consider logically. He gave them more to consider in verse five, "For God doth know that in the day ye eat thereof, then your eyes shall be opened, and ye shall be as gods, knowing good and evil." At this point, they only knew good. The moment they considered the enemy's way of thinking, a new pattern of logic emerged.

God in Genesis 3:9 asked them "Where art thou?" knowing that something had changed, not in their physical location but in their spiritual posture. Their God-conscious innocence had been disrupted by this new logic, opening the door and becoming the catalyst for Adam to eat from the tree which he was told not to.

Sin (behavior) accrues a debt (Matthew 6:12), payable only in blood (consequences). How our sin debt was paid in the Old Testament was by daily, seasonal, and annual killing (sacrificing) of animals. Because of our wicked shaping (Psalms 51:5), sin is always with us therefore we will always accrue a debt we can never escape (John 3:6-7; Galatians 5:19-21). Jesus came as the fulfillment of our sin debt (Matthew 5:17). Sacrifices were no longer needed, and grace had now taken its place (new logic).

Artificial consequences are consequences that start out as neutral but can be exchanged for established reinforcers. An example of this would be a token economy, a method of using neutral items such as poker chips, paper clips, marbles that are exchanged for reinforcers (things the person wants or does not want to do.) An individual would earn/collect the tokens to be later exchanged for reinforcers previously established.

THE INTENTIONAL LIFE

The reinforcer must be established beforehand to ensure the individual is working towards an established goal (reinforcer/prize). For a child, it could look like they are earning tokens to spend the weekend with a friend or to choose the family vacation venue. The method here is simple. It teaches that we can have whatever we want. It is just a matter of how much it will cost and whether we are willing to pay the price. It allows the individual to see the cost-worth relationship and puts them in the driver's seat as to their choices. To be successful, we must recognize we have a choice for this method of consequence.

As believers what we want are the things of God (the fruit of the Spirit) evident in our lives such as healing, loving others, and living a victorious life. We get the fruit of the Spirit by consistently exchanging our old habits for new ones. We must exchange our current filters (standards/habits) for the righteousness of God. That means giving up the prearranged scenarios we have in our heads (feelings, thoughts, and/or assumptions) when we are presented with situations (e.g., trials, tests).

Romans 12:2 reminds us to "Be ye transformed by the renewing of your mind." How we transform our minds is by allowing the Holy Spirit to "guide you (us) to all truth" (John 16:13). We exchange our truth (wicked shaping) for the truth He has guided us to.

The logic of artificial consequences is the template for how we as believers make this exchange. We earn tokens by growing in faith through studying the word of God. We exchange those tokens for the previously established reinforcers with the fruit of the Spirit when confronted with the trials of life.

The reinforcers are why we are willing to "study to shew [ourselves] approved" (2 Timothy 2:15). They are how we show our proof to a righteous God that we believe. Our application of His word is also proof of what we have to look back on and share with others when the next situation arises. Those testimonies are how we are able to maintain during very dark times.

Rarely do we recognize the consequences of our behavior. Either they are delayed and we do not see them or we reject the entire notion altogether by way of a delusion and other means. The word of God tells us in Galatians 6:7 that "whatsoever a man soweth (behavior) that he shall also reap" (consequence). We shall reap. In other words, there is no question of there not being a consequence. The question is how many consequences.

An immediate consequence immediately follows a behavior; they are also the best in recognizing in relationship to our behavior. If you are running and you fall down, running is the behavior, and falling down is the immediate consequence. If you fall and slide and then hit your head, you face additional consequences, but all the consequences are easily connected to the behavior.

When we tell a lie the immediate consequence is the immediate result of the lie. It may get us out of the immediate situation, but that may not be the only consequence of that behavior (lie). Look at David in 2 Samuel, Chapter 11. David was the King who should have been with his men "…at the time when kings go forth to battle…," but chose to stay home.

One evening when he was not able to sleep (antecedent), he decided to go onto his roof (behavior). While on the roof he saw a woman (Bathsheba) taking a shower on her roof. King David sent one of his servants to get her. They slept together, and a child was conceived (consequence).

David then tried to hide his adulterous act by having her husband, Uriah, come home to sleep with his wife so it would be presumed the child was his. When that plan did not work because Uriah refused, saying "…I will not do this thing," King David had him killed in battle. Once Uriah was dead, King David took Bathsheba as his wife.

Although King David repented for his sin, in verse 14 of chapter 1, he learned the child would not live (additional consequence). Not only did King David lose his son, but his consequences also continued even after he repented. As a result (consequence) of what he did in secret, God said He would allow the same thing to happen to David in public. His "wives would be given unto thy neighbor," and God would "rise up evil against him out of his own family," (2 Samuel 12:11). The fulfillment of what God spoke showed up years later in David's son Absalom (2 Samuel 16:20-22). This is an example of what delayed consequences look like and how we lose sight of their connection (a dot) to our behavior. The fact remains that consequences immediately follow our behavior.

Once we lose sight of the order (Antecedent, Behavior, Consequence, or ABC) of the situation (e.g., choice, belief) we lose our perspective of the truth. In the example of jumping off the roof, the antecedent is the disbelief in the law of gravity, the behavior is jumping off the roof and the consequence is hitting the ground. Considering the order of things, we would now look at our recognition of the relationship between the consequence (falling to the ground) and our disbelief in the law of gravity (antecedent) to decide our next course of action. This is how we connect the dots to see our pattern of behavior.

We also choose to see or not see the ABCs by how open we are to things shared with us via the people around us. God uses individuals as vessels to speak to or move through. In Acts 9:17-18, we read about how God through Ananias restored Saul's sight. Saul's physical sight was restored when Ananias laid his hand on him. Had Ananias not gone to Saul and placed his hand on him, Saul's sight would not have been restored. Ananias had previously heard of Saul and his plight to imprison or kill those like him. He had to consider the consequences of his disobedience (behavior) had he chosen not to go.

Challenges to what we know are always forthcoming, but we make a choice, consciously or unconsciously against them, activating or disengaging our blinders. Blinders are a form of self-protection we have. They allow us to function without addressing what we cannot or will not deal with immediately (e.g., situations, concerns, ideas, behaviors, even God).

Why did God give us the ability to block Him out? It is simple, He gave us choice. God wants us to choose Him. The ability to make choices and consider consequences is one of the things that separates us (humans) from animals. Animal choices are dictated by their nature or instincts.

Choice is multi-tiered. The lowest tier of choice is making a choice between things that are similar, narrowed down to one category. An example would be choosing between which fruit tree to eat from in the garden of Eden, (Genesis 2:9) or which dress to wear out of four options.

The next level of choice includes similarities and contrast. This choice includes choosing between our fruit options (similarities) and if we want to add protein (contrast). The addition of the protein changes from a narrow category to a much wider one.

This level of choice requires additional thought as to the consequences of the addition in relation to a fruit-only diet.

Finally, we reach what we will call the ultimate choice, two choices in direct contrast to each other. This is the level of choice from which God appeals to us. In Deuteronomy 30:15, God gives us an ultimate choice of life verse death. Life and death are in direct contrast with each other, choosing one says you go against the other. In Joshua 24:14-15, He gives us the ultimate choice of serving Him alone or other gods.

Making a good or bad choice is when we weigh our consequences against our choices. We have the consequence in mind as we gauge whether it (choice/behavior) can work for us or not. When we choose to activate our blinders, we are choosing to avoid the reality of the consequences we are blocking from our thinking. It does not mean it does not exist, it just will not exist to us and its consequences (random dots), we will not connect back to our behavior.

This activation of blinders (nonexistence) process is temporary according to 1 Timothy 2:4. God wants all His creation to "come to the knowledge of the truth," even when we have chosen otherwise. 1 Timothy confirms that at some point the existence concealed by our blinders will be challenged. At that point of challenge a choice will need to be made, giving way to continuing with the same previous consequences or a new consequence of a different choice.

If we do not acknowledge the consequences of our behavior exist, we will still deal with the consequences of our choices. Even when we do not recognize our choices, when we do not like our choices, and when we allow someone else to choose for us, the consequence will still follow the behavior. Without this acknowledgement, our job is that much harder in connecting the dots of our behavior-consequence relationship.

CHAPTER 4
Hearing the Voice of God

God is always speaking. We just have not been taught to listen for His voice nor do we recognize His voice. He speaks through His creations, His people, His word, visions, dreams, and situations. The sound of His voice can be audible, intuitive, or a whisper. However, most times when God is speaking it is not an audible sound like when we are talking to each other.

The voice of God is very opposite to that of our iniquities. It is very soft and quiet. God speaks in whispers! It must be a deliberate effort if we want to hear from Him, a deliberate effort to quiet all the noise of our iniquities. We must intensely desire and be willing to concentrate our thoughts on hearing His still small voice (1 Kings 19:11-12.)

God is not loud and boisterous like what we are used to in our iniquities. He knows what He has to say is worthy of every effort we put forth to hear Him. At each step in the process of listening, we are rewarded with intense confirmation, but we may not readily trust it. Knowing this, God provides for our lack of trust with His love through grace.

His grace does not condemn us, but it gives us the freedom of acceptance. Acceptance is the conduit through which we flourish. It sets precedence (filter) for self-exploration within the boundaries of His love.

He does so by acknowledging and answering our emotional and psychological nonverbal cries. An example of this is when Moses stood trapped between the Red Sea and an approaching vengeance-filled Pharaoh.

In Exodus 14:15, God is asking Moses, "Wherefore criest thou unto Me?" In the previous verse, Moses is a pillar of strength and faith saying to the children of Israel, "The Lord shall fight for you." Where is this cry God is speaking of that is coming from Moses? There is nothing written that shows Moses is crying out, especially from the children of Israel's view.

Although Moses showed confidence in front of the Israelites, he had no idea how God would save them. He knew he trusted God and His power, but God had not yet revealed His plan. Moses stood before the children of Israel confident in what God said to him but crying out silently in prayer. No one heard the cry of Moses except for the one the petition was intended.

Standing in front of the Red Sea, Moses cried out to God. He had to be thinking we are stuck, and Pharaoh is quickly approaching. His cries were based on what he was looking at with his physical eyes. He had never been in this particular situation before, in the middle of two impossible views. In front of him was the Red Sea and behind him was Pharaoh and his army.

In response, God spoke His instructions, "Go forward!" When God speaks, He expects us to move (be obedient). He had already equipped Moses with what he needed. Moses just did not know how to use what God had given him. He tells Moses in verse 16, "But lift thou up thy rod, and stretch out thine hand over the sea, and divide it."

Who would have thought to do that? Moses had used his staff previously but never like this. He had no idea how to get what God intended without instructions. God used a tool of Moses' trade (shepherd's staff or rod), something he was already familiar with and skilled at using. As we can see, another reason for seeking the voice of God is to accomplish the things of God.

Had Moses not had previous encounters with and trusted God, this scene could have been drastically different. Hearing and recognizing the voice of God is imperative for those seeking to please Him.

Moses, just like each of us, had to learn what it sounds like to hear from God, how to trust what he heard, and how to obey what he heard.

Three steps are involved in hearing the voice of God: He gets our attention, we must respond in interest, and then He speaks. Each step is contingent on the one preceding it, and all must be met. Should we not respond, God seeks out another individual (Luke 19:37-40).

God will and does speak under different circumstances. This is just a guide for learning and making distinctions of His speaking. Once a pattern of His speaking is clearly established, we notice Him speaking more. As the clarity of the pattern continues, God then moves us to a different level of His speaking (Isaiah 43:18). We notice Him speaking more because now we are waiting for Him to speak, and we are developing a desire for Him to speak to us. As this desire grows, we are more apt to listen for Him to speak, and we now have an assurance that He will.

The fact that we came to Christ is evidence that God is speaking. His speaking to us is what drew us to Him. Whether He spoke through a person, our spirit, or a situation, He spoke to us. He continues to speak. We simply must be willing to move as He moves to higher levels in Him, as He calls us (Isaiah 48:17; Isaiah 55:9).

God's wisdom is for those who seek Him and have a listening ear. Although He is always speaking not everyone is listening. For those who are hungry to listen, He provides a smorgasbord of wisdom, as much as our desire seeks Him.

Everything God has to say has value and is worthy of our time. What we do with what He says is vital to our liveliness and the work He has called us to. He tells us in Matthew 7:6, not to give "that which is Holy unto dogs…, lest they trample them under their feet." This is also why Jesus spoke in parables. Those who had an ear for the things of God sought clarity on another level versus the general level of its presentation. The hunger inside their souls demanded more. God knows in advance who will receive Him and when. His grace allows us the opportunity to say no but He already knows.

THE INTENTIONAL LIFE

It is for our benefit that He allows these interactions, so we have no excuse on judgment day. The choice is ours to refuse or accept. Jesus will also not return until everyone has had an opportunity to hear about the gospel of Jesus Christ. Then and only then will He return. During this time of waiting, God is giving us choice and opportunity.

Only He knows when that will happen in accordance with His plans. He is God. He covers all bases, even the ones we do not know about or have not yet thought of. He has made a way for each of us to make a choice to accept His salvation plan or not. We have been given a lifetime to choose. Once we die, the choice we made on earth will be our eternal consequence.

Living this life on earth has its consequences and choices, but salvation is one that we can only choose as we walk this earth. The good news about that choice is, once we make the choice to serve God, we can never be "plucked out of His hand," as John 10:28-30 confirms. Our salvation is for us to decide, and clearly hearing from God aids in that decision.

Even before we are able to recognize the steps of His speaking in our listening, God has already been preparing us to hear His voice. He leaves connections (random dots) or clues in our life's journey that connect to a path we will see in hindsight. Those dots are confirmation of His preplanning in our lives.

He takes special care and attention in revealing Himself to us so that we have proof of His existence and a tangible testimony to share with others. The Bible is a perfect example of this sentiment. It is full of testimonies of His existence, and how and what He did or allowed to bring them about. Not only does He want us to "know" Him, but He also wants us to trust Him. Connecting those random dots throughout our lives reveals a pattern of His consistency, which makes trusting Him more realistic.

He, the Omniscient God that He is, knows that we need a crumb trail (revelation) of who He is before our more formal meeting, and He specifically designed each of our trails with explosive connections that only we can connect with. These connections may be pointed out by others around us, but the confirmation key that unlocks the path to the next connection, God has locked inside of us.

As these locks of confirmation are unlocked, they connect seamlessly to the next, providing us with what is needed to continue the path laid before us. That is not to say that we will not veer off the path like a dog when it spots a squirrel. It just gives us recognition of familiarity, which is needed after our prodigal time.

In retracking Moses' life, Moses was saved from death as an infant when all the other male infants were being thrown into the Nile River (Exodus 1-2). He was raised in the palace by Pharaoh's sister as her son, getting the best education and sustenance. However, Moses ran from Egypt to Midian, escaping retaliation for killing an Egyptian slave master who was beating a Hebrew slave. There he met a Midianite priest who had seven daughters whom he assisted in watering their flock. He was given one of the daughters of the Midianite's priest to wed, and was provided housing and employment by the priest. As time passed the Pharaoh in Egypt that wanted him dead died, and it was now time for Moses to be formally introduced to God.

One day while he was leading his father-in-law's flock along the backside of the desert of the Mountain Horeb, Moses encountered what God had preplanned to get his attention, a burning bush (Genesis 3:2). Whatever God has planned to get our attention, we need not be concerned if it will work because He knows exactly what will do the trick and how to pull it off. It will be a significant event that will not be forgotten nor will the significance of it be lost on us.

God knew where Moses would be, his mindset, the time of day he would be close enough to see the bush, and what it would take to get his attention. He knows how to get our attention and when He predestined each of us for His plans. How He gets our attention is tailor-made for our individuality. He is the one who made us, therefore, He knows how we will respond to what He does, speaks, or sends.

After He has gotten our attention by presenting us with a situation or an option, we are in the driver's seat. We are now the ones needing to decide: Do we ignore His call or answer it? In Exodus 3:3, when Moses saw the fire but the bush was not being consumed, he decided, "I will now turn aside and see this great sight, why the bush is not burnt."

Moses showed interest in seeing why the bush that was clearly on fire but was not burning. By his making the choice to show interest in wanting to know more, he unlocked the door to hearing more from God. He could now hear from the Living God who made him for such a time as this. At that time, the one who protected his life twice to bring him to this meeting, on this mountain, was now speaking to him. Looking back over his life, Moses would connect the dots of how God provided for him from birth to this point in his life. His situation in Midian, of escaping death again after killing an Egyptian, are all evidence of God in his life.

The steps to hearing the voice of God are identical to the steps He took Moses through in Exodus 3:2-5. The first step was on God. The one wanting the change is responsible for making the first move. To modify someone's behavior, the one desiring the change must do something first to initiate a change in the other person. If nothing in the relationship between the parties disrupts the flow of their current pattern, nothing will change. God knowing this knew He had to make the first move, which He did by setting a bush ablaze (Genesis 3:2).

God will always yield to His chosen vessel (us) as to how He moves forward with His plans. He gives us the choice to say yea or nay as to if we will do His bidding. It is not that any one of us can or will stop His plans, He simply wants a willing participant. Once we show interest He further speaks, giving as many details as He chooses using His former pattern of leaving a crumb trail to where He's calling us.

No greater confusion is as clear as the call of God from inside of us. It is something our intellect wants us to doubt but it is familiar without recognition. We recognize the instruction, but we will say "Something told me," or "The thought just popped into my head."

When God speaks, He does so in the same cadence and flow as if the thought were ours. The only difference is we fully recognize the thought was not ours. We struggle because we have seen movies, pictures, and sounds of what we think He will sound like which we associate with Him. Those associations unconsciously become filters that build a foundation of what we think He sounds like when and how He could speak to us.

This is like knowing how to ground yourself during the chaos of a panic attack. The chaos being restrained through the grounding technique are the emotional and physical body shakes that normally flow freely.

Grounding teaches a person to focus on the reality of the present by concentrating on our five senses. It asks us to focus on the things around us that we can see, smell, taste, hear, or touch ("What is Grounding"). While we recognize the wave of panic coming on, we are conscious enough to know to start grounding.

This slight glimpse of consciousness is identical to that of the recognition of God speaking. We recognize them both but neither of them we can control. They are similar because they both are examples of control loss.

As we recognize our lack of control, we seek to understand and pursue the return of the voice at all costs. He continues to draw us to Himself with glimpses and vague wisps of His voice lulling us into a hypnotic shattering of fortified walls built to keep Him out. Challenging our very self-control and sense of safety. Yet reassuring the terror that threatens to send us back to our self-induced bondage.

Finally, we surrender to acknowledgment. It is that balance of consciousness, belief, doubt, and unsure awareness from which we vacillate back and forth, ultimately concluding it is Him.

When we think we have heard from God, we then need to verify what we have heard lines up with His word. For example, we think we heard the voice of God tell us it is okay to get drunk. Next, we search His word for what He has said about drinking (Isaiah 5:22; Galatians 5:19-21; Ephesians 5:18; 1 timothy 5:23) to see if it lines up with what we heard. If it does not, then we know that the voice we heard was not that of God. God will not nor can He go against His word. What He says to one, He says to all (Psalms 23:3; Malachi 3:6; Mark 13:37; Luke 16:17).

He has given us everything that pertains to life and godliness (1 Peter 1:3). He further tells us in Ecclesiastes 1:9, "There is no new thing under the sun." Everything that has been done will be done again. God will not tell us yes or give us something contrary to His word.

THE INTENTIONAL LIFE

For those of us who have things of another (e.g., someone else's spouse) and says God gave them to us, that is simply not His nature. He will not give us something He gave to someone else because of His principle of covetousness (Luke 12:15; Colossians 3:5; Hebrews 13:5).

God can provide us with a spouse, a car, health, and other benefits but we must submit to His will and plan for our lives. The question we must ask ourselves is, "Are we willing to do or not do what it takes in our life to receive what He has for us?" The answer to that question is usually yes in words but not in deeds.

We struggle with our doing things (deeds) outside of our understanding because we are led by our desires. Our desires can lead us either to or from God. When they are in line with His perfect will for our lives, He willingly provides.

Rarely will the ways that He provides line up with the way we think things could or should go nor do they make sense to us, initially. If we ask Him for patience, He will allow numerous opportunities for us to practice being patient. Unlimited situations will be sent (or allowed) by God to challenge our current standard of patience. Each situation is an opportunity for us to cry out to God ("seek ye first"; Matthew 6:33) for His wisdom. As we do so, we will notice a reduction in impatience, resulting in more patience.

What we would prefer is for God to physically override all that He has given within our control and supernaturally make us more patient and calmer in situations, leaving Him to do all the heavy lifting and we just benefit. God will not do that because we are to "work out your own salvation with fear and trembling" (Philippians 2:12).

This scripture is not about our eternal salvation, accepting Christ did that for us. It is about walking toward the perfection that is Christ Jesus, the renewing of our minds, behaviors, and patterns, the exchanging of our standards for His. Those spaces in our soil allotted for our choices, ways, behaviors, and patterns must be occupied (seeds planted) and they are, just not with the things of God!

Those crops must be dug up and presented to God so that He may turn them into good (Romans 8:28) because our soil has been inundated with crops that we no longer want to eat from.

No matter the situation we encounter, God has "a way of [escaping]" (1 Corinthians 10:13) from and back into His embrace. James 1:2-3 tells us to "count it all joy when ye fall into divers' temptations, knowing this, that the trying of your faith worketh patience." To say it another way, the testing of our trust (faith) produces (worketh) perseverance (patience). Everything we give God, He uses for His glory, even if we see it as useless.

If we could get this into our hearts and allow the word of God to show us how to break the cycles of patterns we continue to perpetuate, we could live the life that He has predestined for us. He gives us all that He has planned for us, the process of soul salvation every disciple must endure.

Through various filters, we have created ceilings as to how God speaks. These ceilings are built on the foundation of our emotions, and our five senses and we respond to them with astute precision, limiting how we want and expect Him to speak to us.

In sin, we all were conceived and shaped by iniquity according to Psalm 51:5. In that shaping our responses were trained by those iniquities on how to respond and when. Those responses then moved to automatic responses that we never question, establishing filters to support themselves. Those filters fine-tuned the iniquities dominance which built the foundation of our desires.

Recognizing the call of our iniquities and the comfort that they provide is vital to our discipleship. We know the loud sound of unrighteousness, but what we lack is the voice of righteousness. We wrongly assume that righteousness will scream as loud as unrighteousness. We expect it only because it is what we are used to and readily recognize.

We lack the experiential knowledge of God's cadence. There are times when God is quiet in our situations but only in relation to what He has already said. He knows us in ways we do not yet understand or know about ourselves. He will remain quiet for the time it takes us to process and obey what He has already said.

That time of the process is challenging those systems (e.g., filters/barriers) originated by our iniquities.

This challenging process is the initiation of ultimately how our faith develops. It is the struggle between what we know (experiential knowledge) and what we hope for. When we do not know something, our creative minds seek to provide us with an explanation, creating barriers or passageways. This process is the process of discipleship.

CHAPTER 5
From Sheep to Disciple

Why sheep? Have you ever asked yourself why God choose the relationship between a shepherd and sheep to explain His relationship to us? Although we cannot know the mind of Christ, we can look at the similarities.

Sheep are skittish and fearful animals who are unable to protect themselves from their predators. They are slow, dumb, and without camouflage or weapons of defense like claws, sharp hooves, or powerful jaws. Sheep lack the ability to protect themselves one-on-one, so they naturally stay in tight groups (flocks). They have a natural tendency to wander off and when they do they are extremely vulnerable ("What Does It Mean That the Lord is My Shepherd (Psalm 23)?").

Sheep will become restless if they have not eaten and will not drink from fast-flowing water such as brooks or streams. They need a shepherd for their survival. The shepherd is involved in every aspect of the sheep's life from birth to death ("What Does It Mean That the Lord is My Shepherd (Psalm 23)?").

Shepherds have countless opportunities to individually learn the habits, characteristics, likes, and needs of their sheep. They spend their days and nights with their flock.

They name them and defend them against predators even at the expense of their own lives. Shepherds are known to even count their entire flock nightly, much like a father ensuring all of his children are safe and accounted for. Sheep are naturally timid and defenseless animals and need a protector. They work well following a loving committed shepherd ("What Does It Mean That the Lord is My Shepherd (Psalm 23)?").

Mankind shares many of the same characteristics as sheep. We too are prone to wander, and we struggle like sheep to stay on the path. Isaiah 53:6 beautifully speaks of how we just like sheep have gone astray and turned to our own way. We consistently wander off paths set for us whether those paths were set by our parents, employers, coaches, spouse, God, or even ourselves, and we do so internally and externally.

When we do not know something internally such as how to respond, or what is the "acceptable "answer, we wander back into the dangerous streets of our past history (habits). Those streets include habits of lying, blaming others, selfishness, or muscle memory tactics. Whatever happens internally shows up externally in our behavior making our path detour evident. We innately want the plans of God (Romans 1:17-19), but we have a foundation built on catering to our flesh.

We have a sinful nature that demands our attention even to our detriment (Romans 7:5). No matter how much we want to do better, or how hard we try we can never measure up to the standard of God. God's standard is perfection! He knew when He made us that we would fall short. Just like a loving father, He allowed the first couple to fall as their choice, but He had a plan to recover them and every human after them.

He knows our propensity to wander and provided us with a shepherd who would go after us when we strayed and gave up His life for us. Jesus was and is our propitiation or payment for our sinful nature. It is through Him that our sinful debt to God is satisfied. God did all the work. We must simply accept and receive His free gift. Similar to our wandering, we are equally fearful. If you peruse the Diagnostic and Statistical Manual for Mental Disorders (DSM), you will find an exhaustive list of non-exhaustive phobias.

A phobia is an irrational fear of something that is unlikely to cause harm (Osborn & Raypole #) For example, hydrophobia is literally the fear of water.

People with phobias experience intense fear which causes significant distress that can and usually does interfere with their normal daily living. What makes the fear irrational is the fear in proportion to the situation.

Fear is a distinctive human response to danger or a threat of danger. We, just like sheep, are afraid of everything from our surroundings to water, the very thing we need for our survival. Experiencing anxiety while facing an unleashed growling eighty-pound dog is natural and appropriate fear. That fear becomes irrational on the memory of that initial incident, being unable to cross paths with any non-threatening dog.

Finally, we have no means of protection from our predator, Satan. Satan comes to "steal, kill, and destroy" (John 10:10; 1 Peter 5:8). We are no match for this ancient warrior. Our words do not stop him; our threats do not give him pause. Nor does our physical fighting ability disrupt his plans. Just as a shepherd comes prepared with a rod (Psalm 23) to defend his sheep, God has a plan for us to defeat our enemy.

In Ephesians 6: 10-18 we see a list of the armor God has given us to fight off our enemy. The helmet of salvation (Acts 4:12) is protection for our mind. Coming from a foundation of flesh first (Romans 8:8), we must understand that our mindset must change. Continuing in the way of flesh first will not garner God-kind of results.

Our enemy is very familiar with our carnal weapons of warfare and knows they do not work. He understands the way of flesh for he is the wickedness we are shaped in (Romans 8:7-8). He is the conduit through which sin flows and the anchor to which we are tethered.

The next piece of armor is the breastplate of righteousness, not our own righteousness but God-imputed righteousness. It comes with the belief and acceptance of Christ as payment in full for our sin debt to a perfectly righteous God. The consequence of believing and receiving that gift is our faith (Hebrews 11:1) or shield.

This faith shield literally shields us from our carnal foundation (our sinful nature) that has precedence, giving us a choice to choose from versus satisfying our selfish flesh which our shaping did not allow. It also gives us an opportunity to hear the voice of God instead of moving based on our senses, patterns, or emotions. Now is when we have viable options from which to choose. All previous options grew from the same poisonous soil. Options will now develop from God's perfect and righteous soil that was implanted when we accepted Him.

He goes on to give us a belt of truth on which we can support these new choices. These choices will not be familiar to us, nor will they be what we would have chosen. Therefore, they need to be supported by something (the belt of truth), lest they fall away without little to no thought. They will not be anything that makes sense to us as the things of our wickedness would.

The belt also supports the weight of the only offensive weapon we are given, His word, a sword. This sword supports the choices which are supported by the belt (truth). It gives strength and validity to the choices by waving them in the face of those iniquities. The word of God is the sword from which these new choices grow and are supported.

Finally, we are to have our "feet shod in the preparation of peace" and to pray. The enemy is all about separation and discord, the very opposite of Christ. We only understand peace as we have witnessed it in our wickedness, nothing near God's standard.

The peace that we understand is that of self-serving or avoidance. God's peace transcends our understanding into a realm of His glory. As we walk through our lives, peace is something we acknowledge as void of strife, but God's peace is before, during, and after strife. It encapsulates who God is and how He works in direct contrast to our shaping. Prayer brings us to the conclusion of our armor as a support of all the other pieces. Prayer is communicating with the source of life in a way that He designed. He gives us in detail how we are to commune with Him through prayer in Matthew 6:9-13. He teaches us how to honor His Lordship, repent, make requests, acknowledge His provisions, and our responsibility.

How He does this is broken down in the prayer. His Lordship is established as He is our Father and His name is Hallowed. Hallowed means Holy, consecrate, making a clear separation from who we are in comparison. As our Father, He is our provider, caretaker, and overseer of our well-being. His word says He "sendeth rain on the just and the unjust" (Matthew 5:45), standards for all to enjoy.

Providing sunlight, rain, animals, and vegetation ensures that we can feed ourselves. He gave us the ability and mindset to cultivate crops, raise livestock and build housing shelters for our families. He even made a way for us to open the windows of Heaven to reach Him for more (Malachi 3:10).

His responsibility lies in our provisions. As our Father, He is to provide for our needs, which He does according to His riches and glory (Psalms 37:24-25; Philippians 4:19). God teaches in His word how we are to view, use, and share His provisions in Mark 10:17-22.

His will is what is best for us and the recognition of that puts us in the place to receive that which we need. Led by our feelings we neglect our needs for what feels pleasing to us at the time. We feel we need retribution but what we really need is forgiveness.

Forgiveness is the process of eliminating debt acquired. It is the balancing of our sinful nature (our debt) with Jesus's righteousness (our credit) in God's ledger (book of life). The debts are our sins committed which increase our responsibility (liability) owed to a perfect God. Credits, on the other hand, decrease our responsibility to God.

Forgiveness is a gift that we need and a service we give out (our responsibility). It is the give-and-take relationship of life. God gives us forgiveness through our acceptance of His gift of salvation. We, in return, are to do for others as freely and consistently as God has done for us when they sin against us. We hinder our life when we only do that which our shaping has taught us to do. These are the only ways to defeat mankind's predator known as Satan. Even with these weapons, they must be used when and how God has prescribed them. His word (our sword) is the only thing that stops Satan in his tracks and can give us strength and courage. Courage will be needed when we are standing front and center of a bloodthirsty, ravenous, razor-sharp-toothed dilemma (choice). It is that strength of having our sword in hand that gives us confidence behind our armor to stand trusting God's way!

CHAPTER 6
Process

Process is the actual specific steps it takes to reach a specific desired end. It is the necessary steps from a "here-to-there" pattern that directs the desired end. Process builds patterns that are either clear or random. Once developed, those patterns can be replicated or dismantled.

Process is also how fruit is made. To qualify as fruit, it must be visible, edible, and have seeds. Fruit is the tangible demonstration of who God is and His ability. It is what He leaves with us as proof of Himself, proof of our relationship with Him, and a gift to be shared.

During the process of developing the fruit (data, proof, testimony) is where most of us get stuck, disengage, or abandon the process altogether. We are easily distracted, used to immediate gratification, anxious, and process bores us but developing fruit takes patience. What we want is the all-day flavor to come out of the microwave in a minute.

Fruit must be visible! If we cannot see it in some way, how would we prove it exists? Even God, a spirit whom no man has ever seen (1 John 4:12) can be proven because He can be seen. Take for example the wind. We cannot see the wind, but we feel its effects.

God is seen in His word and manifested in real time which can be traced back to His word. In Job 12:7-8, the creatures created by God can lead you back to Him as proof of His existence. The fruit of the spirit in Galatians 5:22-23 are all things that are visible in a person's behavior, interaction, and speech.

Connecting Dots of Pattern For Clarity

In Malachi 3:10, God says "...prove me now...." If we do not believe God exists, take Him up on His challenge. In a worst-case scenario, you are right. In the best-case scenario, the fruit of His word is made manifest in a tangible way tailor-made for us.

Fruit is edible and desired to be eaten. Think about someone you admire. What you admire about them is their tangible fruit. You praise them for their efforts and dedication in developing the fruit you now stand admiring. It could be their toned body, degrees, bank account, growth, or other highly regarded traits or treasures.

We look at them as wanting what they have but not being willing to go through what they went through to get it. We are eating their fruit when we sit at the table of their sacrifices, gleaning their fruit of experience and applying them to our lives and situations.

Finally, all fruit must have seeds (Genesis 1:29). Seeds ensure the fruit can be replicated. They are what is left in us after we have ingested the fruit or what we share with others.

Once the fruit is eaten and ingested, the seeds go through the process of developing more fruit. This process has three stages: The buried or underground stage, the blade stage, and the fruiting stage. Each stage's length and fruit development are determined by the soil the seed is planted in. Matthew 13 gives us the four potential soils.

In the underground stage, we are alone. Others do not get to see this phase of the process. This is the stage where we are in darkness, where we do not see things clearly, and we are asking lots of questions. This is also where death occurs, death of what we thought, believed, and valued. Death to our truth, our habits, and our will.

Of the four soils in Matthew, only one of them left the seeds exposed which produced nothing but food for birds. "Some seeds fell by the wayside, and the fowls came and devoured them up" (Matthew 13:4). An individual with this heart (soil) could be someone who admires an attribute in someone but has no desire to put in the work necessary to see a similar change in themselves.

THE INTENTIONAL LIFE

In Luke 8:12, we read," Those by the wayside are they that hear; then cometh the devil, and taketh away the word out of their hearts, lest they should believe and be saved." This is someone who heard the word and could not remember what was said moments after hearing it. The word was snatched away before it could be buried. The other three seeds had minimal time being buried. The most productive soil was the good soil, the seed that maintained its burial state until dictated by God.

Fruit development in an individual is much the same. Think about when God called you. You entered a different environment from the one you were used to. You asked a lot of questions, and did not understand everything, but ate (consumed) everything offered because you had hunger (desire/treasure) for more. You were seeking a place to put your heart (Matthew 6:21).

The next stage is the blade phase. The blade phrase is the very moment growth breaks the surface of the dirt. In that moment we see the slightest breakthrough, having just emerged from the underground back into the same environment we left but now with truth. And unsure if or how we would be received, or how it would feel if we will be embraced or criticized.

With all those unknowns, we emerge in the blade phase able to identify growth in ourselves. Something has definitely shifted in our logic, but we do not have much trust in it. This is the time of testing or "fleshing out" this new logic in all areas of our lives.

It is like having book knowledge about driving a car without actually driving the car. We have it all in our heads about how it should go and what we would do if and when certain things happen. During this phase, we are proving to ourselves that we have something, and we are applying our new knowledge and getting comfortable with the newness of who we are, learning to apply boundaries, and testing our own limits. This phase is the beginning of our shift, the first signs of life. The blade stage represents newness. Anybody looking at a blade does not know what it will become, they just see life.

Finally, we have fruit! We have a testimony, strength to share, and food (seeds) for someone else to be strengthened by. In Luke 22:32, Jesus tells Peter, "I have prayed for thee, that thy faith fail not."

Grace and mercy are provided for the times we miss the mark or remain stagnate (lukewarmness). Jesus praying for us is what provides coverage, authority, and power as we "work out our own salvation with fear and trembling" (Philippians 2:12). In other words, when we like Peter see the fruit of growth in ourselves, we are to share our experiences and information with others, "not willing that any should perish" (2 Peter 3:9).

The life we live and the process we go through to get there are for us and others. God wants us to share our underground and blade phases experience with others, how we followed God's leading to overcome. He will ignite that which He put in us when we interact with someone He has sent to spark the fuse.

That is the beauty of being an omniscient God. He knows exactly what we need, when, and how it needs to come. He is proactive with every word He speaks, and Jesus' blood is provided for us to do the same. The process of being intentional is the evidence of our walk.

When we neglect to see the patterns of our very own behavior in others, we fall prey to a process of condemnation found in Romans. What this process demonstrates is the process that goes on in our mind that gives us permission to judge. Romans gives us a detailed view of how we do not connect the dots of our behavior, "There is no new thing under the sun" (Ecclesiastes 1:9). We are guilty of what we judge and in denial of what we excuse.

Romans 2:1 presents a pattern (process) of condemning ourselves. It reads, "Therefore thou art inexcusable, O man, whosoever thou art that judgest; for wherein thou judgest another, thou condemnest thyself; for thou that judgest doest the same things." The pattern is first, we are made to know that we are "inexcusable," meaning we have no excuse, nor can our behavior be justified away. Secondly, we are informed of how we are condemned when we "judgest another." Finally, we are condemned (guilty) because we do the same thing we are judging another person for.

The example of the unforgiven servant in Matthew 18:23-30 is an example of our behavior following this pattern. This servant owed ten thousand talents and could not pay. He begged for patience, and he received compassion and forgiveness.

This same servant had a servant who owed him a hundred pence (a lesser amount) and could not pay. His servant also begged for patience but received prison instead of compassion.

The original servant's behavior was "inexcusable" because he did not acknowledge that he was in the exact same position as his servant. When he chose not to follow the pattern of grace set before him by his master, he put himself in a different category than his servant. This is how we consciously or unconsciously place others above or below us as we excuse our own behavior.

He then judged his servant as unworthy to receive patience, condemning him to the fate of being delivered to the tormentors till he could repay his debt. Finally, the original servant made the exact same request to his master as his servant did to him, both asked for patience because neither was able to pay their debt. Instead of giving his servant what he received and breaking the pattern, he stayed within the pattern (previous filter), condemning himself.

The original servant condemned himself when he refused to give that which he also needed and received. Our wicked shaping is the culprit for this behavior pattern. The pattern is laid out before us. Our choice not to acknowledge it does not excuse us from the consequences. As we continue to live and process our way through life, we begin to notice these patterns more and more, learning to yield to them as we recognize our unwanted consequences.

CHAPTER 7
Intentional Defined

To be Intentional is to be purposeful and deliberate. You must pay attention! Not only to what you do but how you do what you do, if you do it, how you feel when you do it, and the thoughts you think when you do it, etc.

Intentional work is intentional. It is not happenstance to be Intentional. It is making purposeful steps led by a desired end. The desired end is the catalyst for the specific details or purposeful steps. They guide the process with the end in sight.

Being Intentional takes our eyes off everything else and demands focus. It is the only way God wants us to move and grow. It is the "how" we are to walk toward the perfection of Christ.

We cannot be Intentional if are not conscious of what we are doing or not doing. To be conscious means to be fully aware of what is occurring and accepting responsibility for what we do or not do. Consciousness does have layers of awareness that impact assumed responsibility. When and if we choose to be Intentional, we move closer to becoming moldable clay in the creator's hands, instead of unyielding concrete.

The first layer is the surface layer of consciousness, where we are aware to some minimal degree of what is going on in the relationship between our assumed responsibility and our behavior/consequence relationship. For example, when we are multitasking, we are aware that we are giving each task attention, but our awareness of our responsibility and our behavior/consequence relationship is not focused on one task to completion.

A person at this level of consciousness will typically not acknowledge their responsibility as it relates to their consequence. For example, if we were texting while driving and hit the car in front of us, we would most likely blame the other driver for our behavior (hitting them from behind). An individual conscious of responsibility would immediately recognize this responsibility first by apologizing. As the driver behind another driver, we have a responsibility to stay a safe distance behind the car in front of us. No matter what the driver in front of us does, we should follow at a distance that gives us enough time to react to whatever they choose, without incident.

Pointing out the other driver's behavior does not negate our behavior or responsibility while we are driving. We say things like "If they had not stopped," or "They should have...."), clear signs we are not acknowledging our responsibility consciously. Accepting responsibility for our actions has nothing to do with the actions of others involved.

This next level is the subsurface level of consciousness. It could be thinking about other things while someone is talking to you or while in church or class. You might miss a few details, but you have the big picture.

Finally, we come to the level of consciousness needed to be Intentional. Undistracted, fully aware, and responsible consciousness. At this level, we are keenly aware of what we are doing, why we are doing it, and how we feel about our doing it, and we accept full responsibility for our contribution to the impending consequences. We do not struggle to communicate how we feel without anger. We are suited up in the armor of God and braced for an impact (e.g., judgment, criticism, praise, etc.). We do not point blame. We openly admit. We acknowledge the connection between our behavior and our consequences, and we take responsibility for our actions.

This is also where one must be situated for true repentance to occur. Just like when the prophet Nathan came to David and told him about a rich and a poor man in 2 Samuel 12:1-10. With his sin spelled out before him, David owned up to his selfish behavior and repented.

Consciousness does not mean the way or what we choose is correct or the best way. It simply means that we are aware of what we are doing or not doing and acknowledging our responsibility. This level of awareness must include acknowledgment of the potential consequences.

We can choose what comes before the consequence (our behavior), but rarely do we get to choose our consequences. What we do is verbalize an awareness (say what is expected, speak the correct answer) but demonstrate a need (our lack of acceptance of responsibility). Our demonstration whether it be anger, argumentative behavior, excuses, deflection, and the like, shows that we lack acknowledgment of acceptance of responsibility.

That lack of acceptance can be in areas of emotional maturity, discipleship, accountability, or any number of other areas. Another example is when we intentionally choose to not complete an assigned assignment. Our consciousness is our awareness of the potential consequences of our choice (what could happen) if we take this route.

Lack of consciousness on the surface level could be being angry with the instructor, or bringing up how they extended grace to others previously. At a subsurface level, it could be pointing out that the instructor allowed others to resubmit, belittling the instructor's instructions, or an overt emotional response (manipulation).

It is not the instructor who is at fault, even if the instructor had the option to allow us to resubmit the assignment. It is our choice to do it or not. By choosing the behavior of not completing the assignment, we also choose the impending consequence. Our wicked shaping (filter) is to blame, which teaches us to ignore our responsibility.

In 2 Samuel 12:20, David was told his son had died (the consequence for his behavior). "Then David arose from the earth, and washed, and anointed himself, and changed his apparel, and came into the house of the Lord, and worshipped." David accepted his consequence from God because he knew what he had done was wrong. He did not blame Bathsheba for being hard to resist or excuse his behavior in any way. If we believe the potential consequences do not have a role in our decision-making, we may not see our responsibility in our choice, thus, giving us a false sense of reality or a state of unconsciousness.

Every choice we individually make has a bearing on our lives and many times on others' lives. If we do not see the connection between our choice and our consequences, we are not being Intentional nor are we conscious to the degree as previously described. Each choice we make will reveal its consequences and when it does, most of us are unwilling to accept our responsibility.

This pattern of behavior leads us down a self-destructive path of not recognizing the relationship between what we do and the consequences we face, keeping ourselves in the stagnate position of lukewarmness. By doing so we have acquired a taste to pretend that we have no part in what happens to us (activation of blinders) We do so by not acknowledging the choices we make.

Our God is an Intentional God! Isaiah 46:10 details His knowledge of everything that has happened or will happen. When He calls us, He has a reason and responsibility for us to fulfill. That reason is the consequence (ending, result, manifestation, goal) of every step we take guiding us to the fulfillment of His goal. Even His design of mankind was with His goal of our participation in sight.

To learn about a creation, one has two choices: the creation or the creator. The creation can give you some information but only what the creator gave it to give, nothing more. The creator, on the other hand, can give you information the creation cannot. We will look at this process from the creation of a recipe as an example.

The finished product of a recipe is the creation. Reviewing the recipe will give us four things: the name of the dish, a list of ingredients with quantities, a method (how to prepare and complete the dish), and a yield (finished product). This is what the creation has to offer, just what its creator gave it.

The creator of the recipe can give us details about the recipe's development such as why the listed quantities were chosen, what happens if we omit a step, substitutions if we do not have an ingredient, what the finished product should look like, and why or if it needs to rest or cool off.

THE INTENTIONAL LIFE

The same and much more can be said about our creator and His design of us. He is the "author and finisher of our faith" and life (Hebrews 12:2). Everything about us is found in Him including what He made us for, why He made us, to do what, and so much more. Not knowing the answers to why we are here does not mean we have no purpose for being.

God has called each of us to live an intentional life through Christ. He made us for Himself (Proverb 16:4, Romans 11:36, Colossians 1:16) and gave us dominion (Genesis 1:26). God, our creator, provided for us down to every detail, even in the order in which He created us.

Adam (male) was created first, then came provisions (food, career, and residence), and lastly a wife (female). God made the man (male) first in a hierarchical order of His family design, with the husband as the head. Although both husband and wife are equal in our design, we are not equal in our function. God was establishing order for His creation to function.

Females are the only humans who can carry children. We are the weaker vessel (1 Peter 3:7), and we were made for man (Genesis 2:18). God made the decision to make women based on His plan, His goal, and His choice. He is the creator of the recipe; He chooses what it gives.

In 1 Corinthians 11:3, Paul reveals God's hierarchical relationship for man: "I want you to understand that Christ is the head of every man, and the man is the head of a woman, and God is the head of Christ." Each of us is under authority as it pertains to our function. How we are to function in our union is different from our equality of being.

Although they are one, there is a hierarchy in function even in the Godhead. Every person of the Godhead has a role and responsibility. God spoke everything into existence (Genesis 1:1), as creator God. Jesus, God in flesh, came to walk the earth as our example and to be our scapegoat (Leviticus 16:21; 1 Peter 2:1). As our scapegoat, in His death, Jesus released the Holy Spirit to stay with us as our guide and comforter (John 16:7). All three are equal. They just perform different duties as they were designed to function.

God is the head of Christ which is why Jesus was obedient to the Father and said He would only do the Father's will (John 6:38) as He walked the earth. Jesus is God in flesh.

As a son, there is no confusion if He is equal to God. They serve two different functions. Jesus did not question His equality with God. God was and is very Intentional in planning to accomplish His goal as He designed it. In the Godhead hierarchy, He is role-modeling by demonstrating for His creation how we are to function as equals.

In the first five days of creating (Genesis 1:1-23), God was busy preparing what His creation would have dominion over. He mimicked this same purposefulness with the order in which He made mankind and how He told man to live. After God completed what man would have dominion over, He made who would initiate the order in the family, man.

Before Eve was fashioned from Adam, God provided Adam everything he needed to provide for her and any offspring they would have together. God gave specific instructions about what they could eat and what they were not to eat. He also told Adam what would happen if he ate from the tree he was not supposed to eat from. Although Eve ate from the tree first, their eyes were not opened and the fall of man did not occur until after Adam ate (Genesis 3:6-7).

Adam was in "function" as the head, the one ultimately responsible for the actions of his wife and family. He was responsible for leading and guiding his family in the way dictated by God through His example.

Because God gave His creation (man-species) the earth, when it was time to name the creatures, God brought them to Adam (Genesis 1:16-17, 19-25). In ancient Israel, the act of naming an object, place, or person indicated that you held ownership over it (Baraket #).

When God named light and darkness, He asserted His Lordship and control over them for all time (Genesis 1:3-5). The same is true of man (male and female); we belong to God. "We are His workmanship created in Christ Jesus unto good works" (Ephesians 2:10).

God gave man His likeness. We are able to speak things into existence, communicate with Him with or without words, and we are three-part beings just as He is. He expects us to behave in an intentional manner just as He does.

THE INTENTIONAL LIFE

In Malachi 3:6, God says He is God and He changes not. That is what He wants for His creation, to be Intentional and not allow situations or people to move (change) us.

The Intentional Life will challenge us in the way we function and how we move forward. If we allow our own understanding to be put to the test, it will disrupt the status quo! Truth (light) comes to disrupt darkness (untruth/lies), and we cannot remain the same after we begin to seek it out.

CHAPTER 8
Steps to Change

The process of salvation is found in Romans 6:1-14, which speaks about our divine deliverance from sin. No longer are we to blindly do Satan's bidding. We now have another way to respond. That response is not something we are familiar with therefore, we need to learn steps to keep us on the path to becoming Christ-like.

Romans 5:1-11 is a process of how tribulations (things we go through) refine us by processing habits from our muscle memory (automatic response system). An example would be when Jesus went through the process of dying. It was the only time He asked God the Father, "Why hast thou forsaken me?" (Matthew 27:46).

The process of change will be no less painful for us. It involves the removal of ancient trees with enormous root systems and support. The tree (habit) does not want to be removed (die), the ground (soil-heart) does not want to end its role as nurturer, and we do not want to experience the loss of the tree's removal, but we want to change.

Change is the only way to replace the trees of our shaping for trees that produce the fruits of the Spirit (Galatians 5:22-23). Although we want to avoid the pain of the removal, we cannot be transformed (Romans 12:2) without this process. The same can be said about our shaping and the grasp the enemy has on us.

In the creation of life (plants, animals, and humans), God made it so that life could reproduce itself with seeds within it. If the trees of our shaping remain, they continue to produce fruit of their kind. This leaves no other option but removal and replacement.

God's plan for humanity is to spend time in His presence. His goal for us is to enter into His rest with Him and commune. He did the same with Adam until Adam chose to separate himself (bring death) from God by eating the fruit (Genesis 3:6). Communing in His rest is not possible unless we do things His way.

There are patterns or sequences to the things of God. The number three for instance is a sequence of divine perfection. God is a triune God. He made us triune people, and time is past, present, and future, to name a few. Everything has a reason for being and a purpose. Not knowing the purpose or reason does not mean a purpose was not assigned. Every purpose has a process of manifestation. We need to look for the patterns of its development.

We look for patterns in numbers (math), behavior, shapes, etc., and we need to apply that same logic to God and His expectations (purpose in us). That is why the Bible is such an invaluable tool, showing us patterns of God dealing with situations and people to get certain results, and why. Everything is connected like pieces of a puzzle. His word says, "All things work together" in Romans 8:28, not just together but for the good. As we look for patterns, we will understand our Creator more. There are seven intentional steps to this process of change and each step has its own process of matriculation.

Acknowledgment

Acknowledgment is first because it is first. We cannot change something we do not acknowledge, and nothing exists to us unless we acknowledge it. When we acknowledge a thing (e.g., habit, behavior, situation) we bring it into the truth of light, exposing it to the reality of our senses and beyond (spiritual realm).

If we are standing in front of a glass door, we can decide that the door does not exist for whatever reason. As we attempt to exit the "nonexistent" door we will be stopped by the truth of our delusion by hitting the door. It is not that the door did not exist, it just did not exist to us. The door did not exist to us because we made a choice to not acknowledge its existence.

Our reason for making a choice is because we "we were shapen in iniquity" (Psalms 51:5). Making the connection (acknowledging) between our choice and our consequences brings clarity and is a dot of connection to a pattern of our behavior.

Hitting the door brought the glass door into the reality of our sense of touch (pain), where previously this revelation was hidden (did not exist) from us. Until the revelatory impact of hitting the door, we clung to the delusion of our choice. This pattern is repeated as a filter for everything else we do not acknowledge.

When it comes to our feelings, emotions, and beliefs, they too pass through this filter, possibly with more ease because they are within us. They are unlike external challenges (the glass door) in that they can hide behind masks to appear as something they are not, alluding detection.

An allusion is referring to something without actually making mention of what you are speaking of ("Allusion"). It is those hints in our behavior (e.g., fidgeting, no eye contact, avoidance) that tell the story of our secrets hidden away. When children cry to get attention, they do not have the vocabulary to say "I'm sleepy, change me, or play with me," but their behavior shows that they need rest or company.

Not acknowledging something keeps us in the dark longer than we need to be. Our times of darkness have their place (Ecclesiastes 3:1:8), but extending them can be just as detrimental as not allowing them.

When we hold a secret, we have the power to release it or not. The power is in the control of the release and when. For instance, if we are ashamed that we grew up poor, the power in keeping the secret of being poor lies in how we think others will view us in comparison. As long as we keep the secret, we hold back a connecting dot in the pattern of our development.

To acknowledge the true feeling we have about growing up poor unmasks the illusion of strength we originally assigned. How we assign strength where there is no true strength is by putting on a mask (activating our blinders). We give our power (acknowledgment) to masks based on an internal rating that we assigned from faulty filters wrongly installed by wickedness.

The mask only has the power we gave it, and we have the authority to remove it at any time, relinquishing it of its power. If we did not feel shame about how we grew up, there would be no power to hold the secret and we would release it. We assigned it power by labeling the feeling based on the way we felt about it or how we thought we would be perceived.

Feelings are defined as generalized bodily consciousness or sensation, an emotional state or reaction ("Feeling"). They are internal switches we turn on and off based on comparisons and how we view things. They were given to us to control not to be controlled by. Our feelings are where the enemy loves us to lead from.

The fruit of the Spirit (Galatians 5:22-26) is the way of God, but we may not feel like yielding to their manifestation process. When we walk in the Spirit, we put our feelings under subjection to God's perfect will in us. Our feelings may say to get revenge, but God says in Romans 12:19, "Vengeance is mine, I shall repay," which means in His timing and His way.

When we consider how Satan likes to get us alone while going through seasons of testing, we can notice patterns that he uses. Patterns like getting us to think we are alone in our suffering, nobody can relate, no one cares. Alone and isolated, he can manipulate our feelings to come to conclusions that suit his agenda by maintaining stagnate. When we shed light on the things (secrets/feelings) by acknowledging them, we are freed from the shackles of bondage we have called comfort.

Acknowledgment, like most things, has levels of consciousness. The first level is the surface level. This level of acknowledgment is the basic level of recognition with blinders on. It is when our situation does not look like the idea in our head. An example is the notion of youthful invincibility, having an idea but no depth, just a brief acknowledgement.

The second level is the subsurface level or just below the surface. At this level, we have more insight than we do at the surface level. We can recognize behavior in others when we see it, but we make excuses for that same behavior in ourselves. There are tears in our blinders and we are more conscious of the difference between our ideas (stuff in our head) and our reality.

The third and final level is the root or gut level. This level is full acknowledgment. It is here that we accept full responsibility. Scales (blinders) have fallen off our eyes (Acts 9:18) and we clearly see. We have no more excuses. We have full awareness. This is the place each of us must reach in order to fully see. Some have called this place rock-bottom, at the end of your rope, and the like. Seeds may have been dropped for years and now the harvest of fruit (acknowledgment) is ready to be eaten.

Full awareness is required to enter the buried phase. There must be a growing desire (treasure) to recognize that something has to change, something needs to be different. For most of us, this is something that has been pointed out by others previously or we have consistent consequences to refer back to. We have finally made the connection between our behavior and consequences and can identify our patterns of behavior.

This level of acknowledgment is vital because we consistently function out of an area of need or underdevelopment. It is how we allude to our needs. Take, for example, wearing contacts. If we change the color of our eyes, the people looking at us are more aware of how our new eye color has changed our appearance than we are. They see the change, but they do not know the particular details surrounding the change. They just notice a change. Changing our eye color alludes to our need for such things as corrective vision and our lack of self-beauty.

Watching how people respond to our eye color may or may not remind us of the change. We simply go about our day looking through our contacts not aware of what others see. For us to see what others so easily see when they look at us with our new eye color change requires an intentional behavior of looking into a mirror. The mirror is what would remind us of the change we chose.

Until we acknowledge something, it does not exist to us. It is not that it does not exist, it just does not exist for us. As others respond to our new eye color (change in us), they will bring it up, point it out, throw it in our faces, make comments, and avoid or seek us out. They are attempting to get us to acknowledge there is a change or that something needs to change. Others see clearly what we are oblivious to in ourselves.

Until we as individuals acknowledge something is an issue, it can never be resolved. We are the only person who can change us. Not even God will invade our right to be whomever we choose to be.

We all may have heard the question asked why believers do not go into hospitals and heal all the sick, especially when they know in Matthew 10:1, "He gave them power against unclean spirits, to cast them out, and to heal all manner of sickness and all manner of disease." Nowhere in the Bible do you ever see Jesus going to a "hospital" or leprosy colony, because His word says in James 5:14, "Is there any sick among you? Let them call."

There is a responsibility on the individual to do something. If we want something, anything from God, we must make that request known. God gave us dominion and choice, and He will not take them back. It is up to us to learn to access what He has done for us by coming to Him. Acknowledgment is the start of that process.

To move from one place to another requires acknowledgment. Once we come to the revelation that something needs to change, that is when we want to move closer to God. Yes, we can make some changes on our own or within our God-given ability, but when we seek the things of God we must operate as He dictates.

In the stages of process, acknowledgement is when we go underground. It is how we get to that final level of acknowledgment, the root of gut level. The surface and subsurface levels are accomplished before we submit to His leadership, but the root or gut level requires supernatural intervention and being Intentional in the two previous levels.

This underground (buried stage) revelation work is only done between us and our maker. The hand of God is what is needed to pull the weeds (trees) of filters of wickedness from the garden of our hearts. He alone can identify each individual tree within the forest of our shaping.

If our trust has been damaged, the seeds of those wounds have produced fruit of its kind in the soil of your hearts (Genesis 1:11). Those seeds over the years of our development have been watered and nurtured internally by filters and externally by individuals who support those internal filters (James 1:15).

In any area, there may be a couple of trees or a whole forest. How we have traditionally dealt with these trees is to do landscaping by making excuses, "Everybody in my family is this way," "Everybody cheats," "This is just who I am," and the like, leaving the trees intact. Making these types of excuses is a clear indication that one has yet to reach the root/gut level of acknowledgement. This individual still has blinders on and is unable to clearly see the relationship between their consequences and behavior.

One could argue that they do see the relationship between their behavior and its consequences but do not want to do anything about it. This would be an example of a person who is delusional about either the relationship between their behavior and consequences or about their behavior or consequence. To acknowledge one absent from the other is not the required level of acknowledgment.

Those trees (behaviors/filters) have been producing fruit for years and have assisted in establishing our character (fruit) foundation. God must be allowed to pull up each tree, root, and all, and only He can do that! The time it takes to do so is totally dependent on the individual's willingness to confront (acknowledge), forgive, repent, and cast.

God's grace makes a way for the hard work to be done but make no mistake, the work must be done and the individual wanting to move from one place to another will need to be fully committed. Again, there must be a sincere desire, something we want. "Where your treasure is, there your heart will be also" (Matthew 6:21). Whatever it is that we treasure whether it is being president, sobriety, healing, no longer being afraid, or other ideas, our heart will follow.

Our treasure is that thing we desire, something we want, a need so great it compels us to move. It really does not even matter what it is, God just wants us to go through Him for the success of it. When we are seeking Him for anything, showing the sincerity of heart, "...O God, thou will not despise" (Psalm 51:17). God wants to know He has our heart when we seek Him. He gets it because it follows our treasure (desire).

God knows all things, so He knows when we are at the surface level of acknowledgment asking for something that requires gut level. It is like saying we want chicken from Publix deli but only from Publix on the corner of Orange Grove and Hancock because that is where the person we like works in the deli. Our true desire is to see the person in the deli. We are just willing to buy chicken to see them. Instead of being honest about wanting to see the deli staff, we denied ourselves the opportunity to be honest (acknowledge) with ourselves, feeding our habit (behavior) to lie.

Now that we have allowed the tree of the previous pain (old treasure) to be identified and plucked out, the healing of the ground (soil) of our hearts can begin. During this healing process, the word of God will need to be applied often to soothe the soreness and bring peace and comfort. We will now begin to see things in a new light as we enter the next phase of the process of change.

Illumination

Illumination follows acknowledgment. It sheds light where there was darkness. Once acknowledgment has been made and we have stepped over into the process of change, we cannot remain in darkness.

When we accept Christ as our personal savior, we first heed the call, that is acknowledgment. We are acknowledging that we heard, felt, and/or sensed the call of God in our spirit. We then submit to teaching and training, "He that followeth me shall not walk in darkness but shall have the light of life" (John 8:12).

As we remained in our buried stage, our eyes have long adjusted to the darkness, and now slivers of light are forcing us to squint. The light that is causing us to squint is the illumination of connections being made. We now see the connections between the forest in our hearts and the consequences of our life, connecting the past to our present.

Things that were once hidden from us are now visible. The walls of our protection are cracking, and light is seeping in. This is what it looks like when God illuminates in complete darkness and how He feeds the hunger of our treasures. This is when we have answered the knock at the door of our heart and God has come in to sup with us (Revelation 3:20).

The safety of the underground cocoon with God only is where we relax in the comfort of His love. It is where we embrace His unconditional love in our capacity. The perfectness of the experience allows healing in our very soul (Hebrews 4:12). It is only in that perfect place that we allow ourselves to be who we truly are without worldly self-protection.

We need God to illuminate those areas in our lives that we have gone blind to. He sees all and He knows all. He is waiting on us to seek Him out. Just like the GPS systems in our cars, they can take us anywhere we want to go. We just need to tell them where we want to go and trust their instructions enough to follow.

Trust is one of those areas in us that have been so greatly affected that even when we turn our GPS on, we still try to lead. Unlike God, the GPS will re-route us, but God stops and waits. He waits until we realize we took over His job. Remember we asked for His help. We must allow Him to show us how to get what we want or where we want to go. It is abundantly clear we (you) do not know how yet we continue to do when God says, "Rest, I got you."

Clarification

Once God has illuminated our darkness, we can now move into the stage of Clarification. Clarity brings us closer to the blade phase. The light has been turned on, and we are walking toward our exit. Clarity is natural when light has been shed. Think about when we walk into a dark room, we have no idea what is in the room, if someone is in the room, or how the room is set up. Once the light is turned on, we have the answers to all those questions immediately.

Illumination brings clarity which is what forces the blade from its dark place. The newness of life is emerging, connections have been made, and things that were not clear, finally make sense. We are able now to stop ourselves from reacting and "seek first the kingdom," (Matthew 6:33) to be intentionally proactive.

We still have the impulses but now we have insight into making choices from a different foundation. Whereas before, we only had one foundation (wickedness/flesh) option, light has been shed on the possibility of another option (the perfect will of God). This is where testing is initiated.

Clarity of vision and light can expedite our movement in areas more swiftly and more assuredly. Grass comes straight out of the ground it does not peek out to see who is watching. It just shoots straight out. The world the blade is entering, if not ready, must prepare for it because it is coming.

It will not ask permission to exist, it simply exists because its creator gives it permission to exist. When we are clear about who we are and to whom we belong, just like grass, we will simply exist and not look for permission from others to be whom God has predestined us to be. We will walk the streets of the earth with the strut of a lion. Lions fear nothing, not even other lions. They conquer the space they desire. Clarity puts us in that same vein of progress.

Intervention

When we can clearly see the problem (e.g., what does not work, what needs to change), we can then choose to do something different, and Intervention can be inserted. Intervention is what disrupts the current flow of a pattern of a habit needed for change. It comes to shake things up.

Now that the blade of grass has made its appearance and it is no longer underground, it has different needs. The world we retreated from has not changed, only us. We have been resurrected into the newness of life (Romans 6:5) and that new need is why intervention is needed.

Prior to the acknowledgment of change, there was not an agreement on a specific need. Things were occurring as "normal." The new need emerged to say, "I want something else, something different." The previous (prior to underground) status no longer will satiate this new growing hunger. Although it looks like grass, that growing blade (new need, desire for change, treasure) can grow to be tomatoes, and tomatoes must have their vines supported. The weight of what they produce is heavier than the vine they are attached to. When we emerge from the cocoon of darkness, we come with newness that we did not have before.

In breaking habits, intervention does just that, causing an interruption to the way things had been going. It changes the course of action or pauses us to give us enough time to see an alternative. We have acknowledged that something needed to change. We have allowed God to shed light on the situation which has made things crystal clear. Our current course of action will not bring us to our desired consequence. It is the new action of intervention that will yield the fruit we desire.

If we want to stop smoking, acknowledging that we want to stop is the initial seed that gets buried in the soil of our hearts. That seed is watered by the things we allow into our gates (e.g., ears, eyes), illumination is occurring. As light is being shed on the effects smoking has had on our health, finances, family, and other factors, it becomes more and more clear that we made the right choice to quit smoking.
Practice

Practice is when we intentionally disrupt a pattern of behavior with intervention. For example, we can utilize possible aides such as chewing gum, or wearing a patch to assist us in breaking the habit of smoking. The patch would be applied to our arm to gauge its strength to dissuade us from smoking. Practice is also a time to try various interventions until the perfect one is identified for the specific behavior pattern disruption.

It is during this time that we will face our greatest challenge. Remember the old habit is in our muscles. It is a part of us and has been far longer than this new option. The old habit has its place firmly locked down and does not want to be evicted.

Practice is choosing hot or cold and refusing to stay lukewarm. This is where the enemy will fire his most lethal shots, and where battles are won or lost. Our old habits will have our entire body fighting against this intervention.

Getting to this place of practice has been a long and trying journey and it is at this point where weariness appears, but "...be not weary in well doing..." (Galatians 6:9). Weariness is a fork in the road. Do we continue with our new path of intervention or fall back into stagnation of our muscle memory? Facing this crossroad is where we need to do as Peter did in Matthew 14:22, when he said, "Lord save me." Jesus also said, "Come unto me, all ye that labour and are heavy laden, and I will give you rest" in Matthew 11:28.

To receive the rest that God provides we must trust Him and His methods. What He is offering to give us is something we must choose to take (starving our old habits), His yoke, and to learn of Him. Whether we want to accept His yoke or not, we all have a yoke on us. The question is do we want the yoke of this world system (wicked shaping) or that of a merciful loving Father. Either choice puts us back at an acknowledgement of something we want.

This is how the process of being Intentional works. We can never take our eyes off the prize (goal). Any time we do, we risk losing a connection to a particular pattern.

The intentional process is like having a tick on our skin. Either we leave the tick in our flesh (remain stagnate) risking Lyme disease, or remove the tick as soon and as safely as possible (apply intervention). If we choose to do nothing or do not notice the tick, the tick has time to feed on our blood and infect us with any number of diseases it may be carrying in its saliva. In the same way, the tick is infecting us, and so is the wickedness of our shaping.

In either choice we make, we are acknowledging our situation at the surface or subsurface level. Both are a starting point at the fork in the road of a decision. We must be vigilant about staying focused as we walk through this life. Ticks (behaviors/seeds) are everywhere, and they all need to feed on us for their survival.

Simply not being aware of our surroundings or what we allow into our gates (e.g., eyes, ears) exposes us to the ticks of this world system. The longer it takes us to notice one has latched on, the more damage they can do to our entire body.

At this point, we begin to acknowledge that we have chosen to go in this new direction (intervention) and then proceed with getting our mindset, spirit, body, and emotions to line up with it. Once we reach the root/gut level of acknowledgment in this new stage of practice, then we will see progress or be able to surrender to rest. What we are resting in is the finished work of the cross that Jesus died for us to have.

CHAPTER 9
Relapse

Relapse is the next step in the process of change. It is going back to the old pattern of habit. This step is just as necessary as each of the previous steps. Relapse is giving us permission to make mistakes. It is the step where we have significant work rejecting or starving our unwanted habit of behavior. This is the step where we must consistently pay attention to the things around us, how we feel, our mood, etc. It is when we decide to remove the tick but as we do the pain involved in the removal is halted, leaving it intact.

Habits are embedded and they require consistent intentional actions to dislodge them. We will go back to a habit even when we want something different (Hebrews 6:4-6; Hebrews 12:1; 1 Peter, 2:11; 1 John 1:9). They have that automatism about them that without being Intentional we go back to them.

When we buy a new home or move, we may use the GPS system for the first couple of times we go to the new home. Using the GPS system is the purposeful and deliberate step that will bring us to our desired specific goal (new house).

If we are on the phone or distracted in any way and not paying close attention, we can find ourselves far from our destination (headed back to the old house). We have a history of traveling to our previous address. It is an automatic response associated with the old home since we have gone to the new address just a few times.

THE INTENTIONAL LIFE

This process will happen until we learn to trade one habit for another. Our brain is an advanced recall system (Trafton #). The recall slot for going home was created in our brain at the point of leaving our home. Once the space was created by leaving the house, our brains automatically store those things (landmarks) we see, hear, and smell as we pass by.

As long as we have the need to return to this location, there will always be a link in our brain to recall to get us back there. The link is created to meet the requirements of the need. Another way to look at this is from the point of view of God as our source. As our source, He uses several different resources (links) to provide for us. If we incorrectly label a resource, we will struggle when it is no longer available (not needed).

For instance, if we identified our source of provision as our place of employment prior to our underground (death/burial) stage, once we emerged, in our resurrection (blade phase) we will recognize that God is our provider. He was using our employment as a resource (a link) to provide for us (Philippians 4:19). Confirmation is found in Psalm 24:1, "The earth is the Lord's." God owns everything.

While Jesus walked the earth and needed to pay taxes, God provided supernaturally for Him. Jesus sent Peter to a lake to retrieve the tax money from a fish's mouth (Matthew 17: 24-27). When we believe, then "all things are possible" to us (Mark 9:23). Faith is the currency we need to please God. Relapse just happens to be a part of the process of getting there. This process involves a lure (temptation), a fork in the road decision (struggle), and surrender (relapse).

Temptation is the initial phase or the point when options of choice are presented. It is defined as a desire to do something, but it can also be an invitation or a lure. The invitation or lure is based on a desire from within, a desire that is strong or intense and demands action ("Temptation").

"For from within, out of the heart of men, proceed evil thoughts" (Mark 7:21.) For temptation to be tempting to us it must be something we desire. If there is no desire from within us we are not tempted. It is that which is within us that tells on us by drawing out our secret desires. Those desires were concealed from others and sometimes ourselves, that is, until a door is cracked, releasing the demand for action. That cracked door can be initiated by a choice, an invitation, or a lure due to weakened suppression methods.

Our suppression methods are weakened or are relaxed as things around us change and acceptance of our desires is embraced, giving our wickedness an avenue of expression and acceptance that was previously muted. An example of this would be the desire for young girls. In the United States that desire is not widely tolerated under the age of eighteen but in other countries like India, one in five girls are married prior to their 18th birthday ("Child Marriage").

No one can be tempted by something they do not desire. A person who does not desire seafood cannot be tempted by a crab boil. That person has no intense feelings demanding they act by partaking in the crab boil. Even if they are hungry, a crab boil will not pull at their hunger strings. Desire must previously reside within a person's heart to harness its power. Without desire, there is no temptation!

Once the entrance is accessible via the cracked door, that which we are anchored in will jump at the opportunity. This is the point where we must be honest with ourselves and recognize the pull the temptation has on us. This is also where we could ask for help but most do not. We do not because we think we can handle it.

Something to think about when we say to ourselves, "I got this," is "Does it consume your thoughts? Is there an emotional or psychological response (felt in you)? Can you say no and feel nothing?" If the answer is yes to even one of the above, the temptation is too great, and you cannot handle it.

Our prideful wicked shaping is what is saying "I got this." We do not realize how wrong we are until we are too far gone. You may have been known all your life as a fighter, verbally and physically. As an adult, you may no longer get into physical altercations but the desire to defend yourself is ever-present.

That desire to protect determines what type of temptation the enemy sends. Remember our foundation is shaped in wickedness and that is the pool the enemy draws from. That wickedness is the catalyst of our deep secret desires. They arise in many different forms and many different areas, but they always show up.

THE INTENTIONAL LIFE

Those desires inside of us are awaiting the solicitation of a response (demanding action). Although we may have suppressed the desire to physically accost someone, the desire is still evident in the feelings in our body (felt in us) and our thought process (muscle memory). Until that process is interrupted, it will be the link to the foundation (filter) that will always manifest fruit of its kind (take us back).

The enemy will always seek to bring our evil thoughts to a point of action. They bring him glory to see us live our life out of the will of God. Without restraint, void of love for others, and laser-focused on pleasing self, we serve at his pleasure. We tend to not recognize our desensitization as he normalizes perversion. Satan wants us to unleash every evil and deprave thought onto ourselves and others which kills, steals, and destroys us (Mark 7:20).

When we "cast our cares," (1 Peter 5:7) and allow God to heal us, He leaves His love in the slot where our cares were. That love does not jump to defend itself, it just is!

God in His infinite wisdom even has a plan for when we relapse. His word says in 1 Corinthians 10:13, "…But God is faithful, who will not suffer you to be tempted above that ye are able; but will with the temptation also make a way of escape…." How do we recognize the way of escape? This is an intentional act. It is something that we must be aligned with God to be able to recognize and choose.

We may intellectually recognize the way of escape as an option but rule it out as a viable option. Meaning we know intellectually we can walk away from a fight, but our pride filter will say walking away is not an option. Unless we are aligned with God, we will not make the connection to it being our way of escape.

Isaiah 55:8-9 tells us why, "as the heavens are higher than the earth so are God's ways," and His thoughts are higher than ours. We cannot recognize God's wisdom as a viable option in our lives without Him. His wisdom does not make sense to us. It goes against the wicked foundation that we trust. His word tells us to love our enemy, but our wickedness says to hate our enemy more than they hate us. His word says in Matthew 5:40, "If any man will sue thee at the law, and take away thy coat, let him have thy cloak also."

Our wisdom shaped by wickedness tells us to fight back even harder to ensure they get nothing and are left wishing they never tried to sue us. God's appointed way of escape from a disagreement may be to apologize, but if we are consumed with being heard or being right, we will not see or hear that the other person needs the apology (way of escape) more than we need to be right or heard.

God will always require His child to be the bigger person in every situation. Being the bigger person can get old fast if done in our own strength but when we give the result over to God, He will repay. "Vengeance is mine," says the Lord (Romans 12:19). If we do not know His word or are not close enough to hear Him, we will not benefit from His built-in way of escape.

James 1:13-15 points out that no man can say when he is tempted that he is tempted of God. God does not tempt us to do anything nor can He be tempted. He does and will allow tests in our lives but no one can say God tempted them.

The very thought of God tempting us is ridiculous. Not only does God have the ability to do whatever He wants to do to us and through us, He made us, so He knows how we work and how to get us to do what He wants. He "stands at the door, and knocks," (Revelation 3:20), asking to come in. God wants to partner with us. He could have made us robots at His beck and call, but it was His desire that we should have a choice.

 In Genesis 6:5, God saw "every imagination of the thoughts of his [man's] heart was only evil continually." This scripture speaks to the desires in our hearts and they are continual. Galatians 5:19-21 gives further details of the results of our desires or the works of our flesh. Jeremiah 17:9 tells us the desires in the human heart and none of us are exempt. Once we are confronted with what is in our hearts it is the start of the struggle.

The **struggle** is our internal battle between our established filters (e.g., standards, beliefs, understanding, traditions) and that of change (e.g., intervention, innovation). It is the time when the desire is crying out for action, our acknowledgment of it collides. We recognize the necessity of change, but we struggle with the decision to change or not.

THE INTENTIONAL LIFE

That anguish of being sucked back into something we want to leave. The tug of war we have with our emotions and desires (flesh) to do or not to do something different. That wrestling going on in our soul for dominance. Whether it is a behavior, idea, or thought, the struggle is due to one behavior (idea or thought) wanting to dethrone the current behavior (idea or thought) in the position it wants.

Indecisiveness is a struggle. It is the inability to decide or settle something. Comparison also creates a struggle. It is the weighing of the differences and/or likenesses of different objects, people, places, or things.

When we are compared to others, it sets up a standard defined by the one initiating the comparison to both persons being compared. One is better, right, or superior to the other. Both are being defined by the limitations of a flawed individual trusting their own sight (understanding). The only time comparison is accurate is when we are compared to the One who made us. Any other time we are compared to anything else goes against God's design for each of us (Psalms 139).

We lack the foreknowledge of Creator God, in the same way some view Stephen and Jesus' comments as they were dying (Luke 23:34; Acts 7:60). Both men asked Father God to forgive the people in the act of killing them. We in our own understanding (shaping) agree that there are behaviors that are unforgivable. Sometimes we cannot comprehend the concept of forgiving someone let alone forgiving them as they are performing the act to bring about our destruction.

What God knew was that He sent them to die. He chose them for that very purpose. "It is appointed unto man once to die" (Hebrews 9:27). How and when that death comes is only known by God. He does not tell us much of why He has chosen us nor the particular purpose He has chosen us. What He does is calls out to our hearts in a way only He can and awaits our response.

Saul of Tarsus (Paul) who "was consenting unto his (Stephen's) death" (Acts 8:1), was knocked off his horse and commissioned for Christ to suffer for His name's sake (Acts 9:16). Paul did not know when he set out to capture Christians, he would have an encounter with the Living God. Nor did he know that he would suffer throughout the remainder of his life for the cause of Christ.

Although we may not like or understand the plans that God has for us, we must remember that He is not trying to live up to our flawed standards but grow us to His perfection. He does not owe us an explanation as to what He wants to do. Not knowing and wanting information also adds to our struggle of submission.

Struggle can manifest in all areas and in many different forms throughout and within our lives. The same is also true for the length of time we struggle with each situation or decision. Some things we struggle with momentarily, and others we can struggle with for the totality of our lives.

The importance is the recognition of the existence of the struggle process. That recognition affords us the opportunity to process the struggle as quickly as possible, understanding that it is not the process but only a part of the process. Not acknowledging the process of the struggle creates an atmosphere conducive to stagnation.

Connection from one dot to the next ensures a clear pattern. Stagnation halts this process, causing more struggle due to the lack of clarity.

During times of struggle, the enemy is reminding us of how we felt partaking in the act that has now caused struggle within us. He is replaying old feelings, sounds, smells, and all the other pleasurable senses of those times. He wants us to be reminded of those euphoric times so that we overlook the non-pleasurable times (the reason we need change). Giving us memories of elation to return to void of negative consequences. This internal battle wages on in us until one side claims victory. Either we go back to our "folly," (Proverbs 26:11) or we deny our flesh.

The longer we deny our flesh, more distance is created between those moments of elation and unwanted consequences. Those separations allow for patterns to be seen clearly, ultimately making it more conducive to intentional problem-solving. But during the times we are distracted, it will be harder for us to deny ourselves. We will feel the comfort of stagnation during times when we are distracted.

Distraction is anything that takes our attention off of our goal. This includes when we are hungry, stressed, busy, frustrated, and/or tried. In the process of completing any task, we are more successful when we are focused and proactive.

Being focused and proactive on the goal's completion is what propels us to prepare for distractions we know could come. It also gives us the opportunity to think about various solutions and strategies possibly needed.

Imagine deciding to refrain from sweets while at work for one week. Thursday of that week you wake up late (distraction). You leave home without your lunch (distraction), and hunger (distraction) sets in. The doughnuts in the conference room become a temptation. All week you have been able to resist the daily offering because you had healthy options at your fingertips.

Sitting at your desk you notice you are smelling doughnuts, then you hear co-workers inviting you in to join them. Next, your stomach begins to growl, and your head starts to ache. The struggle is preeminent.

We now tell ourselves, "One doughnut will not hurt," or "I have to eat something," which releases us from our commitment to not eat sweets. This initiates stimulation of various neurons in our brains which excites our action-demanding flesh.

Allowing these conversations in our heads is a sign we have decided to move forward in the act. We have made excuses for our behavior, rationalizing what we should do, etc. The desire is already present, making a demand, and we have nothing to fight back with.

God's word has given us a way of escape in these situations, by "bringing into captivity every thought to the obedience of Christ," (2 Corinthians 10:5). While the thought is fresh in our minds we can seek God for help, "yet ye have not because ye ask not" (James 4:2.). Simply asking God and believing (Mark 11:24) that He can do what we are asking for, grants results. His word states, "It shall not come back to me (God) void, ...and it shall prosper in the thing whereto I sent it" (Isaiah 55:11).

As His vessel, we have the ability to speak His word and expect the same. For this reason, we must believe. Our belief is what activates the authority in His word. When we speak His word and believe it, that power is unleashed to manifest that which we are asking for. That does not mean God is our Genie in a bottle but if we ask for things within His will for us, they must come.

The manifestation of the thing also may not look like what we expect. God is higher than us. He does things in the way that He chooses and for our good. Esther chose to go before the king without being called, risking her life. She asked all the Jews to fast with her for three days and three nights, then she would risk it all and go before the King unannounced (Esther 4:11-5:3).

Because she believed that God would provide for His people, she took the calculated risk to put her very own life on the line. She knew not even the King's heart was too hard for God to change to spare her life. Esther left the details of what would and could happen to her in God's hand when she said "If I perish, I perish" (Esther 4:16). Her courageous step is how we get proof that God will do what His word says it can do, and then we can try it!

Esther kept her eyes on the prize of getting the King to intervene. Her struggle was to go or not go before the King unannounced. She knew the law and the potential consequence of being put to death. She struggled with her decision because the King had not called her for over thirty days. Esther did not yield to the temptation to be stagnant, knowing that she might not be spared (Esther 4:13). When we do as she did, believing God will provide, we get a God-kind of result.

Those same internal conversations previously mentioned can also be warning signs for us when we are intentionally making changes in our behavior. They can be the alert that we need to seek God and not entertain them. Matthew 5:28 reads, "That whosoever looketh on a woman to lust after her hath committed adultery with her already in his heart." To use this scripture, we are assuming the self-talk or permission message from inside of us (the man) was issued already. The need inside of him gave him the okay to lust (behavior) based on an unmet need (desire) inside of him. He allowed his desire to explore the unmet sexual desire he had inside of him with the woman in his eyesight.

How we use this as a warning is by acknowledging our own unmet needs in areas of need such as self-control, love, affection, and sex and to question why we are lusting. The next time the sensation arises is the alert to remind us this is an area to give intentional attention to. If we are in denial of our area of need, we will not make the connection between our lust (behavior) and consequence (sin), justifying our behavior with various historical excuses aligned with stagnation.

THE INTENTIONAL LIFE

Even when our behavior is not sinful, we still need to make the connection between our consequences and our behavior to recognize when and where change needs to occur. Just the fact that something we do (habit) does not yield us the results we want is reason enough to review what we can control. The longer we allow the self-talk in our heart and mind, we lean more toward giving in to it.

The struggle is something we cannot avoid. In John 11:21-22, we see how Mary and Martha struggled. Martha is the sister to Mary and Lazarus. Mary is the same Mary Magdalene in Luke 8:2 whom Jesus cast out seven demons and was one of His earliest followers. She and her sister had experiential knowledge as followers as they traveled watching Jesus perform various miracles. They both observed healings and Mary was the recipient of deliverance healing.

With all the history the two sisters had with Jesus, struggle was evident in both their remarks to Jesus after Lazarus died. They both stated "Lord, if thou hadst been here, my brother had not died" (John 11: 21, 32). They both witnessed Jesus restore limbs, sight, and feed multitudes but when it came to their brother they responded out of their emotions.

The struggle presented itself in their words. If He had come, He could have stopped the death, not knowing that He could and was about to raise their brother from the dead. Jesus is all-powerful and His very nature goes against our very nature. We make it difficult unless we are Intentional in our efforts to see Him for the endless possibility that He is.

Just like being distracted by external stimuli, internal stimuli also can hinder our faith as we struggle with seeing (believing) only what we know and can see with our natural eyes. Our understanding or shapening has precedence in our soul (will, intellect, and emotions). The very presence of something different creates conflict for our standards.

Remedy for Struggle

Although struggle is inevitable in our lives, the giver of life can remove the struggle. God removed struggle from the things He made and controls. When He spoke things into existence, He separated them so that there would be no struggle. Light and darkness together were a struggle for supremacy. God ended the struggle when He instituted day and night.

He gave both day and night boundaries in which they could dominate and not struggle for the same time frame. The two coexist without struggle because of the complete decisiveness of their Maker. As humans, we are naturally indecisive due to the fall of man.

God is the all-knowing God. He knows what is best and right. He knows the end at the beginning (Isaiah 46:10). There is nothing that He does not know or catches Him off guard. God as our Maker is the standard of what we strive to be. He made us in His image.

He imputes His righteousness onto us so that we may enter into His presence. It is because of who He is that we received salvation after we fell short. We owe Him our lives for saving us; He owes us nothing.

He has given us a way of escape even in our fallen raggedy indecisive state. If we yield our will to His decisive will, we are no longer indecisive. The problem is when we partially yield but expect fully yielded outcomes. Partial obedience is full disobedience.

God does not adjust His standard to our shortcomings. He made a way for us to meet His standard in our fallen state. It is our job to discipline ourselves to the point we can receive Him His way. He told the oceans where to stop, and they yielded where He said, not a millimeter shorter. Even during a hurricane when there is a storm surge the water always goes back to where it is supposed to be. If only we were as obedient as the ocean.

Relapse is deterioration after a period of improvement, a slip or fall back into a worse former state, or a going back to our folly ("Relapse" #). It is the return to the place we said we would not go back to. Returning to behavior that no longer serves us. The surrendering of our will to that of our desire and sinking back into the comfort of the familiar (stagnation). It is the end of the struggle and the initiation of a new choice. The new choice is present at the point of relapse as to whether to stay or choose to leave again.

Relapse can also be a way we recognize the connection between our behavior-consequence pattern. That same pattern that did not exist to us previously is now made visible. It also provides proof of the hold the previous behavior has on us, demonstrating the need for the Intentional attention required to uproot it.

THE INTENTIONAL LIFE

It is very easy for us to say with words that "something" does not affect us, but others clearly see it does. When confronted with our lack of ability to walk away from it, we cannot deny its stronghold. Denial of the stronghold is how we step into delusion, separating ourselves from reality.

One of the hardest things in the world to do is to try to convince someone of the truth of their delusion. Delusion is their truth distorted by a false narrative that they believe. They will not accept a different version because their delusion is a stronghold.

Ephesians 6:12 reminds us that "we wrestle not against flesh and blood (people) but against principalities, against powers, against the rulers of the darkness of this world, against spiritual wickedness in high places." There are demonic forces behind the stronghold, and they will not relinquish their hold without a fight. An example of this is found in Mark 9:14-28. When the demons saw Jesus they knew it was over but "straightway the spirit tare him; and [he] fell on the ground, and wallowed foaming."

What we must remember is that the battle belongs to the Lord (1 Samuel 17:47). He has given us armor to wear so that we can stand in the evil day (when faced with evil) (Ephesians 6:13-18). Our stance is important because God is the one fighting the spiritual battle. As His representative, we cannot cower and run in the face of adversity. He has overcome this world. He wants us to believe His word, wear His armor, and stand!

CHAPTER 10
Trust

To be intentional we must first trust the process of our development in the hands of our Creator. To do so requires a blind level of trust. Again, process is how we achieve it. Without trust, we have no faith, and "without faith, it is impossible to please Him" (Hebrews 11:6).

Trust is having a firm belief in the reliability of someone or something. It is having confidence, faith, or hope. Trust just like everything else has levels and is routinely compartmentalized.

The level of trust we will focus on is the level of trust that is all-encompassing. This level of trust is when we relinquish all physical, emotional, and psychological control over the involvement of a process. This is the level of trust God seeks for His disciples to have in Him.

It is not something we readily practice or are familiar with. The level of trust we are most familiar with involves worrying, watching, and questioning. When we trust at the all-encompassing level, we are not worried about how the process goes or the outcome. Our faith is in the person we have given our trust.

We cannot have faith without trust. The two are needed to survive. If we do not trust someone, we will not have faith in them (what they say or do.) The hope of our faith lies in the trustworthiness of the person or thing.

"Now faith is the substance of things hoped for…" (Hebrews 11:1). This means our current faith hinges on the thing (a chair holding your weight) or a person (boyfriend) you are hoping to manifest (a proposal with a diamond ring) the desire of your hope (being asked to marry him). We will not have hope if we do not trust the source.

Our hope is sustained by the reliability of the source of our hope, even when the manifestation of what we are hoping for takes time. Our hope remains simply based on the fact that the source is trustworthy.

When and if we find ourselves concerned with a process, we have entrusted to someone else, that is proof we do not trust them at the level of all-encompassing. This level of trust says, "I am leaving whatever happens up to you. I do not need to know how, nor will I concern myself with it. I have full confidence in Your will to know how to handle the process."

Most Christians say we trust God. But what does that really look like? Does it look like the all-encompassing trust listed above? Looking at how we experience life and sickness are great examples to answer this question.

Most of us choose to compartmentalize the things of God to those times in church, church-organized functions, or as it suits us. We can only see Him through the lens we allow ourselves to look through. Without the leading of the Holy Spirit, we cannot walk in the supernatural (Spirit realm).

We readily view our life experiences and sicknesses through our past experiences or wicked foundation. We have what the word of God says in the Bible in our intellect. But do we let it get into our hearts even though it may go against our understanding? Do we allow ourselves to crossover into the victory God has promised us or do we accept defeat?

"For as the heavens are higher than the earth, so are my ways higher than your ways, and my thoughts than your thoughts" (Isaiah 55:9). The key to unlocking the blockage in our minds (hearts) is trust. Everything about being Intentional hinges on trusting the process before us. If that process must be spelled out verbatim and to our satisfaction, trust is aloof.

THE INTENTIONAL LIFE

The Holy Spirit comes to lead and guide us to all truth (John 16:13). That truth will not make sense to us based on our historical understanding. He is a perfect God, and we are far less than perfect. Our work must be in learning to walk from under our standing to His understanding.

For many different reasons, we find it difficult to not only comprehend but also to implement. Everything about Christ's way of living and loving is so far removed from our innate reality. Our brain creates these safety patterns that we learn to trust and strengthen.

We have a wealth of history to compare ourselves to others based on acceptance, worthiness, and every other possibility. We do not adjust well to change. We do not like pain or discomfort, nor do we fair well with correction or chastisement.

We work all of our lives to get to a place of consistency that defines success for us. Breaking those well-fortified habits is not easy to relinquish. Most of them we do not even recognize we have them, yet we want them versus the unknown. The unknown things of God are represented by our shaping as embarrassment, weakness, negativity, and the like.

So, when it comes to demonstrating our trust in God as His word says, we do what we want and not what His word says. We will even say what the word of God says, but we will not discipline ourselves to do what the word says.

For example, Matthew 18:15-17 clearly tells believers what to do if a brother (any Christian) sins against them. Instead of doing what God's word says to do, we make excuses for our disobedience by saying things like "We just do not get along," but not getting along is not an option. We are told to "love our neighbor as thyself" in Matthew 22:39. To love someone is to do for someone, which includes getting along with them in some capacity.

It is one thing to disagree with someone, but it is something entirely different to not be able to get along with someone. To not get along with someone says that neither person is willing to give up the right to be right or to be the bigger person. God always expects His children to shoulder the responsibility of maintaining peace (Romans 12:18.) He even tells us to "love our enemies" in Matthew 5:44. He makes no exception for us to not get along with other people He loves.

We are to go to that brother (person), bring someone with us, and/or go to the congregation, if needed (Matthew 18:15-17). This should be standard practice in every ministry, but it is not. The chief reason has a lot to do with fear and pride.

Another way to look at our trust in God's word is when we are sick. God's word is replete with scriptures about what to do when sick. He told the disciples in Matthew 10:8 to "heal the sick." Then in Isaiah 53:5, we read, "By His stripes, we are healed"

Matthew 10:1 says He gave us power. If we trusted that we have that power, we would do what Mark 11:23 says and speak to the mountain of sickness or anything else standing in our way of doing what God has called us to do. This way of behaving takes intentional effort to move past our habits. Without it we continue the same path of behavior, unchanged.

Trust is formed when we connect to truth and are able to test it. Testing is our proof of process to an established end. It is our final result after we have tried many different angles and ways to disprove what we really wanted initially.

Testing is beneficial because the human brain is bent towards the negative. We can hear 999 positive words and one negative word. Our brain will automatically focus on the one negative word instead of the 999 positive words.

This negative bent is distinctive to the human brain. It is the standard. As new stimuli (information, persons, situations, etc.) are introduced. They are analyzed against stored pathways to confirm connections or placement. To do anything different, our brains must be trained. This is why Jesus's example of leaving the ninety-nine (Matthew 15:12) to go after the lost sheep is so powerful. It demonstrated the connection and test relationship previously mentioned.

That lost sheep when found by Jesus and carried back to safety, connected to the truth (Jesus and all He represents) in a way the others had not. The rescue demonstrated that Jesus would come, that the sheep was valuable and worthy, and that he could miss the mark (make a mistake). The other sheep may have thought the same, but this sheep had a testimony in addition to what the others had.

Matthew 5:45 tells us that God "rains on the just and the unjust." It is His nature to give. It is what love does (John 3:16). His love is eternally hopeful that we will choose Him and He made what He made accessible to all enemies or sons. It is in our hands to seek more if that is what we want.

The rescue solidified the relationship between that sheep and his shepherd. That sheep had an experience (test) to refer back to should he waver in trusting Christ in the future. The herd did not test the connection they had with Christ. What proof do they have He would do the same for them?

The prodigal son is another example, but this time we will look at the brother (herd), the one who did not leave. Luke 15:29 says the older brother was angry with his father for celebrating his younger brother's return (test). We can all speculate as to the brother being jealous but consider this. The older brother remained at his father's house, never testing his connection with his father in the way his brother did. Was it because he did not think he should, did not trust his father would forgive him, was too afraid to do anything, or lacked self-permission?

Whatever the reason he chose to not test his connection, the result was anger, misplaced anger. The older brother had every opportunity to do as his younger brother and/or more, but chose to place blame everywhere except on what held him back. The older brother's reaction of blaming is an example of how we see fault in everything and everybody except ourselves.

The very reason we train children is to teach them to be responsible for their actions. As parents, we are responsible until they can be. Only in situations of physical, emotional, or developmental deficiencies do we as parents maintain responsibility for our children after a certain age in life.

Building trust teaches us how not to micromanage, how to let go of the details, and how to relinquish someone else's creative flow. This all-encompassing level of trust gives the permission message to an individual or group that they may take a vision, put it through their unique lens, and offer their view of it.

When Jesus said, "Go ye therefore, and teach all nations" in Matthew 28:19, He did not dictate exactly word for word what they were to say. He provided the command (vision/goal/standard). The manifestation has been left up to our obedience to the Holy Spirit. We can evangelize anywhere, at church, at a bank, while playing cards, or even as we are learning to stop smoking. The only requirement for evangelizing is sharing the word of God.

Our job is to plant seeds and water. Christ brings forth the increase (1 Corinthians 3:6). How each of us plants and water is unique to us individually! Even more so when we are led by the Holy Spirit, we cannot get it wrong. It might not end the way we envisioned the situation in your head, but God knew exactly what He was doing when He chose us in that season, for that particular situation.

Only He knows how that interaction with us will lead an individual to the next link in His plan. Someone who has been homeless has shared pain and relatability with those in the process of homelessness. That history puts them in a unique position to connect on a level than someone who has never experienced homelessness. Not that one must have experienced homelessness to reach those who have, it is just an added level of connectedness.

Our willingness to share our testimony of our past homelessness could be just the thing a person needed to hear to push them to make the tiniest of steps to turn toward God. That connection could be the door God chose to invite a conversation. Our willingness to have that conversation is an example of planting seeds or watering. Refusing to do so demonstrates a lack of trust that Christ will do His part.

When we say we trust, the fruit of our actions proves it. We must be willing to do as God directs so that He may be glorified. It is for His glory that we intentionally surrender our will (traditions, habits, beliefs, etc.) to trust His plan for our life. Doing so may mean for us, exposure. Exposure can be scary when we have worked our entire life to keep things hidden but again, His glory!

How to Build Trust

For the most part, we all are rebuilding trust. Trust was established and defined long before we noticed our current level of trust. The foundation of our trust was built from infancy and grew and changed in many forms as we grew and changed.

To rebuild trust, at some point we will need to take a leap of faith (Hebrews 11:6). Rebuilding trust requires us to go against what we have believed. We cannot rebuild trust by staying at the comfortable place of trust we currently know. Remember those brain pathways? To rebuild trust, we must create a new pathway.

THE INTENTIONAL LIFE

Creating that new pathway requires going a different way than we want to go, the previous path we have taken effortlessly and without thought (muscle memory). This new pathway requires intentional focus and action. We must sacrifice all that we think, feel, and believe in order to move in a different direction.

However, that decision to go in a different direction will be met with opposition. The strongholds (habits) of our foundation (wicked shaping) want things to remain the same, unchanged. Change means death for them. Just like our fight, flight, or surrender mood takes over when we are threatened, that same mechanism is activated when we initiate change.

We will struggle with voices inside our head telling us all that could happen, and why we should not move forward, reminding us of previous times we tried to do something different that did not work. Those voices are the attempts of the enemy. He uses scare tactics to keep us in place (where he wants us). He wants nothing more than to retain us as his workers of iniquity (Mathew 7:23; John 8:44). If and when we break free from his hold in this area, he knows it will affect every other area he has a hold of in our lives.

During this struggle is where and when we need to cry out to God for reinforcements (Matthew 14:30; James 4:2). God will not do for us what He has given us to do (2 Peter 1:3). He has given us victory (John 16:33)! We need to choose it by faith and activate His finished victory by speaking (Roman 4:17). God will send His hands and feet (willing vessels) to encourage us. but the final work must be done by us (the individual).

"My grace is sufficient," God tells us in 2 Corinthians 12:9. His strength is made perfect in weakness. It is just like teaching a baby to walk. We can help them up unlimited times, but we cannot become their legs and walk for them. They must get up and keep trying against all odds. It is the same for us, we must go against our current trust level into this new unknown, unproven level that God is calling us.

When we are able and willing to do so, we see in James 2:20, that faith without works (steps) is dead as the truth it is. Our faith is the hope we have that God is telling the truth (He's got us), and our work is the demonstration of not standing still when the fiery darts (Satan's scare tactics) come. How we do it is through trusting that God's strength will maintain us as we move past the wall that has stagnated us previously. That, my friends, is how trust is built.

Our shapening has defined our "truths/standards," prior to accepting Christ. Those foundational lies are what must be surrendered, so that the truth of Christ may reign. As our new foundation is being built through testing, we will ultimately resolve God as Truth.

There is only one truth (John 14:6)! As we move closer to accepting the truth there will be struggles. We cannot serve two masters (Matthew 6:24).

The strength of those lies will reveal themselves in our backsliding. Imagine a game of tug of war, two sides pulling in opposite directions. No one side gives in until the winning team has progressed. If you replace the players of your tug-of-war (the vision you had in your head when you imagined tug-of-war) with the enemy and Christ at opposite ends, you still have one side pulling relentlessly, led by our standards (old foundations, behaviors/habits, iniquities). That other side is something entirely different. You see Christ standing there waiting to be acknowledged, waiting to be invited into the game.

As you look at Him, you think, "Why are not you pulling? Why are you not fighting for my hand?" At that moment you hear a still small voice saying, "If any man hears my voice" (Revelation 3:20). Then is when we realize we are expecting Christ to behave like the enemy or how we have previously had our needs met. Christ is different; He does not yell. He does not demand. He simply waits, knocks, and asks.

It is up to us to respond to Him. Throughout this process of recognizing Christ and His methods, we will backslide. The iniquity that we have been shaped in is the lie we have settled for as truth. That shapening is the result of our fallen state which puts us swimming against the current. God's word is the way of the current. Going against it expels lots of energy with little progress.

Backsliding is when we go back to our old way of thinking or doing. To change our habits, we must consistently and intentionally go through the steps of change found in chapter eight of this book. Forgoing these steps leaves us in the same or worst condition than we started (2 Peter 2:20-22).

CHAPTER 11
Pride

Pride is a sneaky little thing that hides right out front in the open. It can be a noble self-esteem that comes from the consciousness of worth to a generous elation of heart. Pride can be an inordinate self-esteem, an unreasonable feeling of superiority as to one's talents, beauty, and/or accomplishments ("Pride"). It can be rude, arrogant, and show insolent treatment of others.

Pride is what gives us permission to treat others as they treat us. It releases us from responsibility while blaming others. It puts the self before others, does not ask for help, and only sees from its viewpoint.

Unlike pride, love denies itself for others. Love says, "I am willing to sacrifice my right to be right for righteousness' sake." Both love and pride are demonstrated. They both emanate from the human heart, and neither is ever satisfied.

It is from the root of pride that we expect maturity from someone based on age and not fruit (behavior/manifestation). The expectation grew out of our (the individual assuming) standard of what or where we assume a person should be based on his or her role, title, age, gender, etc.

We naturally expect women to know what to do when they give birth. We expect the elderly to be wise because they have lived thirty or forty-plus years longer than us. When we assume maturity based on preconceived perceptions, we miss out on what is displayed before us.

THE INTENTIONAL LIFE

Pride can be what keeps us from growing in the areas God is working out, in, or through us. It says, "I am good. I do not need that pressure. This is way too much for me." And then it causes us to give up. Pride is the reason why the brother of the prodigal son was so angry in Luke 15.

He deflected the responsibility of his internal feelings off on his father. His father was excited to see his younger son return but the brother thought a celebration was not worth it, although the older brother received his inheritance at the same time as his younger brother (Luke 15:12).

The older brother accepted no responsibility for how he viewed his relationship with his father, his father's relationship with his brother, or his relationship with his brother. Pride gave him an outlet for anger by avoiding the responsibility of managing his feelings and relationships.

Pride says, "I am the only person who can do it right!" It blinds us and gives us permission to remain in deceptive darkness of ourselves and those around us. David saw nothing wrong with his behavior until the prophet Nathaniel came to him with a scenario of someone else's prideful behavior. Once David saw his sin from the vantage point of an onlooker, then he could see the sinfulness of it (2 Samuel 12).

Then and only then did he see his behavior for what it was. Just like David, we are the last to know who we really are. Pride affords us that luxury. Again, we are busy manifesting our behaviors and we have eyes that see out not inward.

It takes an intentional effort to see ourselves as we are versus the vision we have created in our heads. Pride keeps us laser-focused on others in comparison, so we do not see ourselves as we truly are. We can be so blinded by our position, title, and/or unchecked behavior patterns to the point of complete delusion.

Matthew 7:5 reminds us to "Cast out the beam out of thine own eye; and then shalt thou see clearly to cast out the mote out of thy brother's eye." We tend to only focus on others with criticism and ourselves with praise. Our gifts can take us places our character cannot keep us. If our character does not catch up to the vastness of the platform God has brought us to, it can be the very vehicle of our destruction.

Pride is one of those weapons the enemy uses that we make excuses for in our lives. To the point, we give pride a place of honor in our lives and when the word of God comes to challenge it, we have a ready excuse. "I will not change for no one," or "I have always been like this." What about when we accepted Christ, "Old things are passed away; behold all things are become new?" (2 Corinthians 5:17). What happened to the new? When does the new take over if the old has precedence?

The word of God comes to challenge everything about us. In Matt 10:34-36, Jesus said, "I came not to send peace but a sword." That sword is to sever ties with our prideful will. There is no other way for our will to disengage without it.

The word of God offends the things of this world. They are at enmity with each other (James 4:4). If the word of God does not offend EVERY area of our life, we are not applying it to our life. We sit down at a table in front of our enemies in verse five of Psalm 23. That table is to show our enemies who God is in our lives and what He is able to do through us in their presence.

When Jesus came to earth, He knew exactly why He was coming and for what reason. He knew Judas would betray Him, when and how. None of that information that Jesus knew allowed Him to show Judas any less love than He showed the other disciples (Matthew 26:50.)

If we accept the premise that each of us does not readily see our own behavior, then we would acknowledge that we must accept someone else's view of us. We know that they would see the areas in our lives that may need attention (change) clearer than us.

The same is also true about others seeing our beauty, gifts, and skills that we have not noticed. The union of marriage is the greatest example of this. When husband and wife join in matrimony, they see themselves through the eyes of their spouse. They each can look to the other for areas in their behavior that they do not see.

Marriage in the Bible is defined as a man and a woman (Genesis 2:18-24). Another way to define the union is that of opposites. Men and women are opposite in many ways. Men are the givers of seed and women are the receivers of seed, women are communicators, men are typically not, and the ideas of femininity versus masculinity are just a few ways we are different from each other.

In the process of becoming one, the two individuals are learning to fuse together their individuality to function as one. They have the opportunity to test their uniqueness, shed their outer protective mask, and learn vulnerability on a deeper level. Each person takes responsibility for building the oneness they both seek in their union.

Pride is the reason we tend to think of our behavior as not an issue. It is also why we prefer the company of those like us who will not challenge us in areas we need a change in. When a spouse is put in a position of not being heard by their spouse, it separates the union of oneness, allowing the enemy to have his way with both individuals in ways neither are intentionally watching for.

Their individual focus is now on what and how the other is behaving. They are ignorant of the works of the devil (2 Corinthians 2:11). They, just like us, focus on the individual and not the source (root) of the evil.

The enemy comes to "steal, kill, and destroy" (John 10:10). How he does that depends on the access we allow him. We give him access through our disobedience to Christ and through our will.

Satan is an ancient warrior who has supernatural powers (Ephesians 2:2). He knows just where and whom to use to come into our lives to do the most consistent damage. While we are fighting with each other, he is gaining a foothold in our hearts (Ephesians 4:26-27). He is applying just enough pressure to keep the couple not speaking, not praying, and isolating themselves.

He creates a wedge between them that ignites a blame fest. Pride is Satan's favorite weapon because it is right in our face, but we do not see it. We all know intellectually none of us are perfect and we all make mistakes. Although we know this information, we still will not concede to hearing each other.

Pride has initiated a tug of war. Once the tug-of-war has started it is no longer about what started the fight but winning at all costs. We do not see it coming nor do we acknowledge it.

Until we see the enemy for who he is and not the person he is currently using, he does not need to use any new tricks. Pride is working very nicely for him. "We wrestle not against flesh and blood" (Ephesians 6:12).

Satan only uses tactics that work for his agenda. He does not even have a very large arsenal because the ones he has are so effective. He simply rotates the few he has, and they consistently prevail in our relationships.

Instead of focusing on the deception of the situation, we as people tend to only focus on the individual, losing sight of how the enemy has gained a foothold in separating the union and our power to speak to the situation. Leaving the couple emotionally scarred, drained, hopeless, and ripe for destruction is the enemy's goal. He comes to kill, steal, and destroy, not to make uncomfortable. Once he kills the togetherness, he continues to fuel our minds to steal what is left, ultimately annihilating the union altogether.

It is the mirage of the mountain that takes us over the edge, and we simply give up. Instead, we could allow the voice of God to penetrate the walls we have built around our hearts to come down and drain the ocean of pain we have gathered over the years. Forgiveness would have a chance to settle the tornado of feelings, giving us the opportunity to see clearly.

Seeing clearly is the remedy for the tsunami the enemy has inflicted. To see one's way to the truth of the word of God is the only way to move beyond what hurts. If we can just get to the shores of God's love, we can rest. His word tells us in Matthew 11:28, "Come unto me all who labor and are heavy laden, and I will give you rest."

It does not matter how we get there, once we are there we can stay as long as we want and come as often as needed. When we are ready to leave, He continues to provide for us, "Take my yoke upon you and learn of me" (Matthew 11:29).

Christ wants us to learn how to live in this world with our hearts set on pleasing Him. To do so we must be willing to be taught how to surrender our way (our will) of handing things to Him. The Intentional Life is the tool for the job of our initial steps.

"Vengeance is mine, I shall repay" (Romans 12:19)! "How does God repay?" you ask. Just look at Judah in Genesis 37:26. Judah did not want to shed his brothers' blood, so he suggested selling him into slavery.

He with his brothers deceived their father and Tamar deceived him (Genesis 38:13-16). God allowed Judah to reap what he himself had sown. God does things in His way and in His time. Accepting His sovereign will and His timing is what must be done.

Pride is the part of our will that conflicts with a desire to surrender. The opposite of pride is humility. In every situation, we all have an opportunity to present either one. Just as life and death are always before us as a choice, so is pride or humility.

Death and pride we are more familiar with and make more concessions for. They are both of this world system and come naturally to us. Remember we are shaped (molded) in iniquity.

The law of first mention is the idea that the first time something is mentioned in the Bible will be the simplest and most understandable reference from which the others build ("What Does It Mean That the Lord is My Shepherd (Psalm 23)?"). God moves us from level to level throughout our lives, which grows us up in maturity. The more immature we are, the less we will recognize pride where a higher-level maturity is needed.

Teachers are taught to teach students based on this concept. It is the reason we matriculate from grade level to grade level. The goal is always to get the student to the highest level of thinking as quickly as they can retain and conceptualize the information.

For instance, let us look at sharing. Sharing to a small child may simply mean giving my brother some of my candy or letting my sister play with my toy. At that stage of development, it may not include the length of time they give the toy to the other child. The child may allow their sibling mere seconds to have the toy in their hands before they snatch it back.

In their underdeveloped minds, they have done what was asked of them. Yes, in that second instance, sharing occurred, but the goal is to teach or lead the child to the fullness of what sharing is. Sharing requires denying self for the good of the whole.

Learning to share is a foundational stone of getting to, "By this shall all men know that ye are my disciples, if ye have love one to another" (John 13:35). "How so?" you ask. If we cannot share, we will not comprehend the basics of God's love. His love is unconditional. It forgives 490 a day (Matthew 18:21-22). His love is eternally patient (James 5:7). His love says if our enemy is hungry, we are to feed him (Proverbs 25:21-22; Songs of Solomon 8:6-7).

Learning to share is part of love. "For God so loved the world He gave" (John 3:16). He shared Jesus with the world and all its inhabitants (John 6:38). God sacrificed His only begotten son for the sake of His enemies, us (Roman 5:8; 8:7; James 4:4-10).

Couple that with 2 Corinthians 9:8, He likes a cheerful giver. God wants us to give cheerfully and willfully of ourselves and the resources He provides us. Until we reach a level of maturity, we cannot and will not accept this line of thinking. Our lack of maturity will not allow for it.

Applying the law of first mention to our behavior as to how we were shaped in iniquity gives us a starting point. Our first exposure to a particular behavior builds precedence (a seed planted) in us. That precedence leads the way and charts the path for all that will come behind it. As the precedence is validated and confirmed (watered) by observations and demonstrations, it creates a well-worn passageway solidifying its position.

When a man and a woman come together to conceive a child even before the child is born, they influence the child. If the mother is worried, stressed, or fearful she passes that unsteadiness onto the child. Just as the child steals nutrients from its mothers' body, they also absorb her emotions which is evident in infants who struggle to sleep, nurse or stay asleep ("When I Feel Sad While Pregnant, Does My Baby Feel Sad?").

The child is a spirit first which is housed in flesh and directs its soul. The spirit is what makes us a person and is subject to the ways and atmosphere we surround it with. Our spirit is released at the point of conception.

As the body of the child develops through the stages of life, it is shaped by what it interacts with including other spirits. Every interaction we have is anchored in the spirit world. The child feels what its mother feels, and its spirit is shaped by her emotional responses and those she allows around her.

Once we "seek ye first the kingdom of God and His righteousness" (Matthew 6:33) to deal with the spirit realm, that which is visible (what we see) has just lost its life source. Imagine a balloon being filled with helium or when a flower being cut from its stem (root). Once the balloon comes off the helium nozzle or the flower is cut, its life source (helium/root) has been severed. The balloon nor the flower can sustain its life without the source that gave it life.

THE INTENTIONAL LIFE

The same is true with the things we see that impact our lives. Whatever is causing us issues (success or stress) is being fed from the spirit world. Once we sever that connection between the spiritual realm and the earth realm, the thing that is visible (a situation, person, etc.) will end. Some things will be immediate, and others will slowly die.

We can at least look at them differently by allowing our thoughts to be influenced by the word of God. Doing so can remind us we are in the process of doing our first works over (Revelations 2:5). We are relearning to do things the way God says to do things versus how we were initially shaped.

To put it into other words, the individual the enemy is using as the point of our stress will no longer be our point of threat (Ephesians 6:12). We can simply love the person and speak to the spirit (Mark 11:23), allowing our anger to fuel our prayer and study life. As we do so we will have unlimited opportunities to speak the word to our situations and watch the manifestation of God (1 Corinthians 3:7).

Our prideful habits of confronting, medicating, or avoiding will be challenged. These challenges are necessary to give us opportunities to "… work out your own salvation…" (Philippians 2:12). It is in the "workout" or practice that we exchange one habit for another.

Continuing in the way of our habitual previous patterns (pride) only produces fruits of the flesh. When we submit to the new way (intervention), we disconnect the root from the flower (that which is visible), killing it. This frees us to experience how it feels doing things differently. If we do not try something new it does not matter how well our landscaping is (excuses, not disconnecting from root), the root will produce fruit at some point again.

Think about how we see the same things occurring over and over in our lives. Everywhere we go we deal with the same things. We consistently attract the same type of people. We routinely have identical situations repeated with slight variances.

The cycle is repeated because we have not killed the source of light (the root of pride) that sends out communication from your soul saying, "I need you." Instead, we are saying out of our mouths, "I do not want to deal with this type of person, situation, etc.," but the source (root) of the beckoning has not yet been extinguished. If the root remains intact, it will ALWAYS reproduce its kind. It cannot produce anything else.

This "scary" root work is the reason we give over to our habits for a temporary reprieve, a reprieve from the thought of doing something different. In the reprieve, we go back to the way we have been, a place where we know how to survive.

Continuing in this way causes us to doubt, not trust, make more excuses, and the like, giving our pride leverage that the enemy can and does use against us. Our behavior will only change when the spirit (root) of that which is causing the behavior is dislodged.

To have faith in the process would be to practice the new intervention. The intervention for pride is humility. James 2: 17 reads, "Even so faith, if it hath not works, is dead, being alone." Our faith must be accompanied by works!

Our work is taking steps to walk away surrendering our understanding to the One who knows all. Every step we take toward Him makes it easier to take the next one. God will "never leave thee nor forsake thee (us)" (Hebrews 13:5), but we must move in His direction.

While the child endures the behaviors of its parents' faith, patterns are left behind of belief and unbelief. How we as individuals manifest these patterns (habits) is as individual as we are. They (habits) are so embedded in us that we do not even know why we do the things we do. Therefore, we hear people say they are finding themselves, which we all are, but where are we looking?

If we allow our own understanding to direct us, we give our guidance over to our pride. Pride will direct our search for ourselves to evidence that supports its agenda. Remember pride is sneaky. It will have us looking at a mirage of a water fountain, encouraging us to drink. As we bend to take a drink of the mirage pride created, it floods our minds with thoughts of how refreshing the water is.

Our subconsciousness will confirm the refreshing water because we have had water before. However, a mirage of refreshing water does not refresh thirst in that moment. A mirage (or vision) can be all we need, especially if it is to draw us closer or it is something to walk towards.

Psalm 139:13 (New King James Version) reads, "For you formed my inward parts, you covered me in my mother's womb." We cannot go to the creation (e.g., man, nature, animals, stars) for things only the creator knows, that is if the truth is what we seek. When and if we do, we are left frustrated, more confused, and further away from God.

God wants us to know Him and His plans; He simply wants us to come to Him. Pride on the other hand does not. Pride says, "I do not need to go to God. I can figure it out myself." God's desire is to have a relationship with us and for us to live life to the fullness of joy. To do so, we must "seek ye first the kingdom of God" (Matthew 6:33).

His desire for us is clearly laid out in His word, we just do not believe it. We do not believe it because of the lies built into our prideful foundational shaping. The truth of God's word must fight against those stronghold lies that have precedence.

For if we forsake the law of Christ, we forfeit His knowledge (Romans 3:20-31), therefore, leaning on our own understanding and falling deeper into a prideful situation. That situation leads to the destruction of self, which is the goal of only one, the enemy. We get caught up early in the lie of the enemy by not submitting ourselves to be taught the truth of the word of God. As this continues, it shapes us at the foundational level of whom we grow into.

Children suffer the consequences of their parents' gifts, knowledge, shortcomings, and other behaviors. When a child moves out of their parent's home, they have an opportunity to test their own limits. We do not truly know what we will do until there is no one around saying what we can and cannot do.

Outside of their parents' limits, the child now has an opportunity to learn to disciple themselves in a way their parents could not or did not. Most adults who think they were raised in a "good" home may not readily see their needs, unlike those who were raised in foster care, drug homes, domestic violent home, or single-parent homes.

It does not matter the conditions of the home we were raised in, we still need to correct our foundation to be a vessel for God. None of us are perfect and "all have sinned and fallen short" (Romans 3:23). When we can look at our lives from this vantage point, then we are on an even playing field with everybody else.

God is a spirit and everything He produced continues to produce its kind. He does not continue to give instructions to what He created. When He speaks, in His voice is all that is needed to sustain and reproduce life. Humans are His only creation that can rebel or defy Him.

We are the only creation He gave free will. We have volition of our will to do as we please even to our detriment. We can reserve the right to change our mind as Naaman did in 2 Kings 5:1-19, to refuse or comply. We are "His workmanship" (Ephesians 2:10), designed and crafted just as He wanted us to be.

When we make use of the gifting, skills, and abilities God has given us, we are able to do the things He is able to do. Not in our own selves but through Him (Philippians 4:13). His desire is for us to live a life of abundance (John 10:10)!

He made it so by giving us the remedy for success. James 4:10 reads, "Humble yourselves in the sight of the Lord, and He shall lift you up." If we would only humble ourselves and allow Him to teach us how to live in His kingdom, we shall see success.

The most dominant way that we are like God is also what hinders us the most, the fact that we are dominant in nature. When God placed the first man, Adam, in the garden of Eden, He said let them rule (Genesis 1:26).

Remember the law of the first mention? We were designed to rule, and we want to rule everything, everywhere, and all the time. We take great pride in having control over things and people.

This is how pride has been able to grow to uncensored levels of normalcy and acceptance with little to no backlash. We have a natural capacity to rule, and we struggle with discipline. Discipline is what separates disciples from failure and/or success.

THE INTENTIONAL LIFE

A disciple is a disciplined one, one who submits himself to be taught or trained. The Bible tells us to train our children, to study, and to assemble ourselves (Proverbs 22:6; 2 Timothy 2:15: Hebrews 10:25). When we refuse to do so, how can we call ourselves disciples?

Let us look at the life of two men named Saul. The first one became king. This Saul was going about his business doing what his father told him to do, looking for donkeys. The people of that time wanted a king (1 Samuel 8).

God told them through His prophet what would happen. He told them how the king would take their land, property, and children for his use (1 Samuel 8:11-17). They still wanted a king because they wanted to be like the other nations. Because God gave us dominion and free will to choose, He gave them what they wanted (volition of their will) instead of what He wanted for them.

Saul had no idea he would be the chosen King. He was busy doing the will of his father. Creator God created a crossroad with the prophet Samuel and Saul. Samuel was told by God who he was to anoint Saul. When he saw Saul, God confirmed that he was the man.

Saul was given the position of the highest in the land (1 Samuel 9). As king, he made a crucial mistake that took him out of God's favor. Instead of killing everything and everybody like God told him to, he decided to be disobedient to God by keeping the best sheep, cattle, and King Agag alive. Saul's act of prideful disobedience cost him his kingdom. His lack of discipline was made manifest when he did what he wanted to do versus what God said to do (1 Samuel 15).

The next Saul is Saul of Tarsus who was knocked off his horse on the road to Damascus (Acts 9). This Saul also did what he thought to be right by killing and imprisoning Christians. He fully believed he was doing the will of God. Until God, Himself asked him, "Why persecutest thou me?" (Acts 9:4). Pride can convince us that our way is the right and only way. Submitting ourselves to Godly teachers can challenge even the longest-standing views we have harbored.

Disciplining ourselves is just the beginning. It is the start of our intentional process, not the end. This intentional process gets us in a position to give over the reins to a very capable and loving God.

Connecting Dots of Pattern For Clarity

The Intentional Life process we have walked through was just to get us to a place of surrender. A place where we could acknowledge the things we could not or refused to see. It was to allow a time of focus to engulf us in the things of us, that we would see ourselves in our wretched state of being. It was simply to get us to a place where we can clearly see our need for Christ.

Without this intentional process, we would continue in our thinking that we are "good people," further missing the mark. God is calling us to a higher place. Completing this leg of the journey puts us in the most optimal position to cry out to God, to recognize our great need for a Savior, and to surrender our will more consistently to the One True God who created us.

Works Cited

"Allusion." Merriam-Webster.com Dictionary. https://www.merriam-webster.com/dictionary/allusion. Accessed 22 Feb. 2023.

Baraket, Elinoar. "What's In a Name? The Bible vs. the Middle Ages." TheTorah.com. https://www.thetorah.com/article/whats-in-a-name-the-bible-vs-the-middle-ages. Accessed 22 Feb. 2023.

"Child Marriage." UNICEF. June 2022. https://www.unicef.org/protection/child-marriage. Accessed 22 Feb. 2023.

"Desire." Merriam-Webster.com Dictionary. https://www.merriam-webster.com/dictionary/desire. Accessed 22 Feb. 2023.

"Feeling." Merriam-Webster.com Dictionary. https://www.merriam-webster.com/dictionary/feeling. Accessed 22 Feb. 2023.

"When I Feel Sad While Pregnant, Does My Baby Feel Sad?" Regional Medical Center. 6 Aug. 2020. https://rmccares.org/2020/08/06/when-i-feel-sad-while-pregnant-does-my-baby-feel-sad/.

How Are Diamonds Formed? Diamond Nexus. https://www.diamondnexus.com/blog/how-diamonds-are-made/. Accessed 23 Jan. 2023.

Osborn, Corinne O'Keffe and Crystal Raypole. "Can I Be Afraid of Phobias?" Common or Unique Fears Explained. Healthline. 3 Jan. 2022. https://www.healthline.com/health/list-of-phobias#:~:text=A%20phobia%20is%20an%20irrational,a%20certain%20object%20or%20situation.

"Pride." KJV Dictionary Definition. https://av1611.com/kjbp/kjv-dictionary/pride.html. Accessed 22 Feb. 2023.

"Relapse." Psychology Today. https://www.psychologytoday.com/us/basics/relapse. Accessed 22 Feb. 2023.

"Temptation." Merriam-Webster.com Dictionary. https://www.merriam-webster.com/dictionary/temptation. Accessed 22 Feb. 2023.

Trafton, Anne. "How We Recall the Past." MIT News | Massachusetts Institute of Technology. 17 Aug. 2017. https://news.mit.edu/2017/neuroscientists-discover-brain-circuit-retrieving-memories-0817.

Webster, Jerry. "ABC: Antecedent, Behavior, Consequence." ThoughtCo. 28 Aug, 2020, thoughtco.com/abc-antecedent-behavior-and-consequence-3111263.

"What Can Trees Tell Us About Climate Change?" Climate Kids. NASA, 20 Dec. 2022, https://climatekids.nasa.gov/tree-rings/.

"What Does It Mean That the Lord is My Shepherd (Psalm 23)?" GotQuestions.org. https://www.gotquestions.org/Lord-is-my-Shepherd.html

"What is Grounding." Psychological & Counseling Services. University of New Hampshire. 14 Feb. 2023. https://www.unh.edu/pacs/what-grounding#:~:text=Grounding%20is%20a%20self%2Dsoothing,and%2Dnow%20and%20to%20reality.

"What is the Law of First Mention?" GotQuestions.org, 15, June 2017, https://www.gotquestions.org/law-of-first-mention.html. Accessed 22 Feb. 2023.

"Yoke." Merriam-Webster.com Dictionary. https://www.merriam-webster.com/dictionary/yoke. Accessed 22 Feb. 2023.